THE FUTURE OF FREEDOM IN RUSSIA

THE FUTURE
OF
FREEDOM IN
RUSSIA

EDITED BY

William J. vanden Heuvel

TEMPLETON FOUNDATION PRESS
PHILADELPHIA & LONDON

Templeton Foundation Press
Five Radnor Corporate Center, Suite 120
100 Matsonford Road
Radnor, Pennsylvania 19087

The opinions expressed in these documents do not necessarily reflect the views
of the John Templeton Foundation.

Special thanks to Declan Murphy and Karen Dinsdale of Impresarios, Ltd.,
Washington, D.C. for their help in making this book possible.

Designed by Richard Eckersley
Typeset by G&S Typesetters
Printed by Data Reproductions, Auburn Hills, MI

Library of Congress Cataloging-in-Publication Data

The future of freedom in Russia / edited by William J. vanden Heuvel.
      p.   cm.
   Includes bibliographical references and index.
      ISBN 1-890151-43-2 (cloth : alk. paper) — ISBN 1-890151-44-0 (pbk. : alk. paper)
      1. Civil society—Russia (Federation)   2. Rule of law—Russia (Federa-
tion)   3. Civil rights—Russia (Federation)   4. Capitalism—Moral and ethical aspects—Russia (Federation)   5. Russia (Federation)—Social policy.
   I. Vanden Heuvel, William J. (William Jacobus), 1930 –

JN6699.A15 F88 2000
323'.0947—dc21   00-031547

Printed in the United States of America
00 01 02 03 04 05 06   10 9 8 7 6 5 4 3 2 1

CONTENTS

PREFACE

THE FUTURE OF FREEDOM IN RUSSIA

WILLIAM J. VANDEN HEUVEL

Mr. vanden Heuvel has served as deputy U.S. permanent representative to the United Nations and as U.N. representative to the European Office of the U.N. Now of counsel to the law firm of Stroock & Stroock & Lavan, he is also Senior Advisor to Allen and Company, a New York investment banking firm. Ambassador vanden Heuvel has served as president of the International Rescue Committee, as chairman of the Board of Governors of the United Nations Association of the United States of America, and as chairman of the New York City Board of Corrections. A graduate of the Cornell University Law School, he was editor-in-chief of the Cornell Law Review and later served as executive assistant to General William J. "Wild Bill" Donovan, special counsel to Governor Averell Harriman, and assistant to Attorney General Robert F. Kennedy. Ambassador vanden Heuvel is a member of the Council on Foreign Relations, chairman of the Franklin and Eleanor Roosevelt Institute, and chairman of the Council of American Ambassadors.

To UNDERSTAND Russia is not only a compelling intellectual experience, it is a necessary commitment if the twenty-first century is to fulfill the possibilities of "a well-ordered society." Attitudes toward Russia define optimists and pessimists, those who see the glass half full or half empty. It is a country whose culture and brilliant achievements in literature, music, and science tell us that given a democratic framework and an assurance of freedom for its people it can certainly emerge as a powerful, constructive, contributing leader in a world where its geography has such a commanding place.

In February 1999, the John Templeton Foundation convened an unusual conference at the Library of Congress. James Billington, the brilliant Librarian of Congress and a major force in the area of Russian studies, gave the keynote speech with an eloquent, poetic invitation to consider the future of freedom in Russia. The invitation itself told us that something very different was at hand – that the pessimistic view of Russia, now the reigning orthodoxy of the American foreign policy establishment, was about to be challenged. Instead of asking "who lost Russia" – the very question bespeaks the arrogance of those who believe that great nations are available for purchase and sale – a roster of participants spoke from the heart and the heartland of Russia, reporting the human dimensions of current problems but also describing the inspiring energy, commitment, courage, and genius of countless men and women who will be the unsung founders of the "new Russia."

What they have to say is worth hearing. Their credibility is contained in their biographical descriptions – imprisoned dissidents under the old regime, men and women of religious faith who survived the brutality of Communist repression and who now illuminate the search for new directions, entrepreneurs whose imagination and pragmatism reflect the tenacious creativity needed to build a prosperous economy, citizens committed to the fundamental freedom of speech and expression knowing it to be the true guarantor of democratic government. They do not deny the profound corruption, the political skullduggery, and the financial mismanagement in contemporary Russia. They know those problems as well as anyone, and their statements graphically describe them. But they report the good news of decency, honesty, and determination that has brought enormous progress, often invisible to those who travel only to Moscow and St. Petersburg, progress often achieved despite of, not because of the national government, progress that is the seed corn for the years to come.

The Templeton Foundation has done something extraordinary in assembling such a group, so very different than the usual array of experts who never tire in telling us everything that has gone wrong. The Foundation recruited presenters largely from the distant regions of the Russian Federation where many of the most interesting political and social developments are taking place. Scholars and grass roots organizers were brought together to give their insight and experience into planning the years ahead. One has the feeling that we have come upon the soldiers in the trenches who, despite remote and listless commanders in the capital headquarters, understand what has to be conquered and have the strength of passionate determination to win the struggle.

Washington policy makers, listen to Boris Pustintsev, the president of Citizens' Watch, a nongovernment organization that works for effective civilian and parliamentary control over Russia's security agencies. His credentials were established when he led demonstrations *inside* Russia in 1956, protesting its invasion of Hungary. He spent years in Soviet prisons and labor camps. Even in democratic Russia he has been a target of the KGB. He talks of history and the process of reconciliation, of a Russia bound to Europe and striving together to overcome racism and bigotry, of Aleksandr Nikitin, whose report on the threat of the radioactive waste engendered by Russia's Northern Fleet caused his arrest and trial for espionage. Mr. Pustintsev's commitment to truth and the rule of law makes his a voice that must be heard if freedom is to have a future in Russia.

With wit and courage, Arkadii Novikov, a creative, very successful entrepreneur, discusses how he conceived and built his chain of thirteen restaurants and the ethical dilemmas he confronted in a Russia "where no businessman can operate honestly." He looks to the new government to establish a legal framework that will both encourage enterprise and integrity. One has the feeling that Mr. Novikov and those like him will do more for the economy of Russia than the planners in the Kremlin.

Father Georgii Edel'shtein, a parish priest in the Orthodox Russian Church, describes the Moscow Patriarchate as "the most reactionary institution in Russia." For twenty years he has ministered to the needs of the poor and oppressed in the remote village of Karabanovo. His words are the essence of the freedom to worship. His faith will move mountains, and maybe even the hierarchy of his church.

In enunciating the Four Freedoms as the basis of the democratic world to which he committed America's strength, Franklin Delano Roosevelt understood that freedom of speech and expression was fundamental to his hopes. Both the government and the oligarchs are a threat to this freedom in contemporary Russia, but when you read the words of Larisa Malinova you understand that a new army is being organized, an army of trained, independent managers and journalists who are prepared to work and fight for media access so that uncensored, accurate, unselfish information can be brought to the people of Russia.

Each writer, each article has a message that is relevant and powerful. The traumatic history of the twentieth century has left Russia gravely wounded. In the transition from Communism, its resources have been plundered and greed has replaced creed. From the miasma, voices emerge that echo the best of democratic values. These men and women deserve first our audience and then our support – the support of our government and each of us individually – support that will give substance to their commitment to a free society based on values of social justice that we share, sustained by allegiance to the rule of law that ultimately defines a civilized community.

Whether encouraging free enterprise, an independent judiciary, the rule of law, a commitment to freedom of speech and expression, or the right to worship as each individual chooses, our government would be well advised to emulate successful venture capitalists: bypass the corruption of the Moscow "apparat," find good people and projects on the local level, carry out proper due diligence, and then monitor progress and provide support to help reach the goal they, the people of Russia, have set for themselves.

Sir John Templeton is a famous optimist whose spiritual faith has been the bedrock of his success. The Foundation that bears his name, in sponsoring this conference and publishing this book, reaffirms his understanding of the complexity of freedom's cause and the moral strength required to achieve it.

PART I

ESTABLISHING FREEDOM UNDER THE RULE OF LAW

BRING OUT YOUR DEAD!

BORIS PUSTINTSEV

Active in the defense of human rights under the Soviet regime, Boris Pustintsev now is president of Citizens' Watch, an organization that unites the efforts of legal experts and human rights activists to bring existing Russian legislation closer to international legal standards. He has worked closely with the American Helsinki Watch, for which he investigated Russian prisons and labor camps, and he lectures widely on human rights, both at home and abroad. In this chapter Mr. Pustintsev discusses the current situation in Russia with regard to human rights and the rule of law.

THE RULE of law has never been supreme in Russia. Notions of freedom and the rule of law stem from the European nations, from a branch of Christian civilization that was alien to the strong Byzantine tradition prevailing throughout the history of the Russian Empire. Beginning with Tsar Peter I, attempts to introduce European practices in Russia historically have come from above. In 1836 the great Russian poet Alexander Pushkin complained that "the government is the one and only European in Russia." Considering that Russia was an absolute monarchy at the time, one can imagine what this suggested about the attitudes of the population.

At the same time, when we discuss the outlook for the progress of freedom and the rule of law in the Russian context, we imply that Russia is spiritually already a part of Europe or that it will be incorporated into Europe in the foreseeable future. There is a historical contradiction here that deserves special attention.

The first serious attempts to introduce the concept of a state ruled by law were made in the 1860s, when Alexander II initiated his reforms. Since then Russia gradually, and with repeated setbacks, has been moving closer to Europe. Democratic institutions were consistently introduced, starting with certain elements of local self-government and extending through the rudimentaries of electoral and parliamentary culture and constitutionalism in the early twentieth century. Principles of legality took root, including the establishment of an independent judicial system, laws of civil and criminal procedure, and trial by jury. The advances in the legal profession were remarkable. Problems of juvenile justice that are a novelty for a majority of Russian jurists today were discussed heatedly in Russia before 1917, for example. Rapid industrial progress dictated further liberalization of society. Though the country remained an autocracy, a certain continuity of political evolution toward Europe was evident.

All these developments were interrupted, then eradicated, by World War I. In early 1917 the monarchy fell, and basic freedoms and liberties were introduced. But the short nine-month period when citizens gloried in the enjoyment of their newly obtained civil rights coincided with the height of the exhaustive and bloody war. In these extreme conditions, the newborn democracy soon proved so weak that the Bolsheviks had no difficulty in forcibly dissolving the first freely elected Russian parliament and usurping power. The consequent chaos of the ensuing four-year civil war erased all the civilizing achievements of the previous half-century and culminated in a dictatorship of the Communist victors. As a result, Russia again moved away from European traditions – for good, the Bolshevik rulers hoped.

Since the collapse of Soviet Communism, however, the country again has turned to Europe. In the past ten years Russia has made a gigantic leap in the direction of becoming a state governed by law. For the first time in history, the Constitution has declared the supremacy of citizens' rights over those of the state, of international legal standards over national legislation. The inviolability of private property has been guaranteed. There are no formal taboos for the mass media. The judiciary has formally gained full independence.

Nevertheless, in modern Russia the adoption of these attributes of civilized states has produced utterly unexpected results.

During their seventy years in power the Bolsheviks systematically destroyed the concepts of freedom and the rule of law in society. Using means of terror, they turned the country into a political and moral wasteland. Therefore, when Mikhail Gorbachev tried to save the sinking Soviet ship by liberalizing the regime, the result was the only one possible in such conditions. Instead of the "socialism with a human face" that he promised, Russia got a democracy with the face of an idiot.

Political, economic, and social reforms in the former Soviet Union were initiated from above by a ruling Communist elite that quickly learned to pronounce, without batting an eye, such phrases as "world civilization," "common values," and even "human rights," though with a distinct Soviet accent. The group of reformers led by Mikhail Gorbachev and Aleksandr Iakovlev wanted to modernize the regime enough to end East-West confrontation, which the country no longer could afford. They deserve their place in the pantheon of reformers: very few leaders of the omnipotent Communist Party realized that the state-run economy was on the brink of collapse. Gorbachev and Iakovlev, however, did not intend drastic changes that would put an end to Soviet rule. Quite unexpectedly, the momentum of events proved so strong that some members of the group of reformers were themselves carried with it.

At the beginning of *perestroika,* the changes were welcomed by the man on the street. People were so disgusted with the previous rulers that they would support anyone who uttered anti-Communist slogans. Any change seemed to promise better things; any political idea not derived from the Soviet catechism sounded like a revelation. When part of the ruling elite realized that events were beyond their control and that the reforms intended to strengthen the regime were undermining it instead, they staged a coup d'état in August 1991. In response crowds of protesters, ready to fight against the return of dictatorship, took to the streets of

Moscow. Despite their earlier willingness to use force in Vilnius, Riga, and Tbilisi, the plotters backed down in Moscow, stopping short of provoking massive bloodshed in the capital. Yet many of the same protesters who in 1991 had defended democracy voted in 1993 for Communists and for the ultranationalist Vladimir Zhirinovskii to represent them in Parliament.

In the months following the aborted 1991 *putsch,* it seemed possible to lay the foundations of the rule of law and make the process of democratization irreversible. The reformers seemed to sit firmly in the saddle, while their opponents were frustrated and frightened. The people who came to power preached civil rights, political liberties, democracy, and a market economy. But nobody bothered to try to solve this simple riddle: Where had all the professed democrats suddenly sprung from? Where had they been so successfully hiding until the last moment?

Just yesterday all these people, with few exceptions, were Communists. Whether they were sincere or cynical in their espousal of communism was irrelevant. Freedom was an alien concept for them; they had long since forgotten its taste. For generations they had been subjected to taboos that everyone pretended to observe but tried to evade in everyday life, and the double standard had become second nature to them. At the same time people had become accustomed to, and wholly dependent on, the paternalistic state that would not let them starve even if they did not lift a finger to earn a living. "Grab what you can today, and the hell with tomorrow" was the general motto. "You can do nothing about the future; you do not shape it." Only the present mattered, because there was no past.

The Communists treated the past in full accordance with the famous formula coined by George Orwell: He who masters the past will be the master of the future. Millions of people in Eastern-bloc countries were professionally engaged in falsifying historical events and in controlling access to information, that is, in controlling the minds and souls of their compatriots. Their efforts were not made in vain. The dictatorship succeeded in destroying the memories of several generations. Those in the former Soviet Union were worst off; their memories were erased over a period of more than seventy years. People lived in an artificial, illusory world, not knowing what really was going on outside their country and in most cases not wanting to know. The Soviet empire fell for predominantly economic reasons, as we know, not because its citizens rebelled against it. They were too skillfully controlled *en masse*.

Even in the Soviet era, however, there were people, albeit very few, who took pains to record any facts related to the events that the authorities tried to falsify or suppress. Harassed and persecuted by the KGB, these people nonetheless carried on their work. They operated in their own underground world until they could come out into the open in the late 1980s as members of the Memorial Society, which united former victims of political repression and their relatives. At that time, the Soviet authorities ignored their demands for access to party and KGB archives. After the failed putsch of 1991, however, the new government yielded to popular pressure and opened part of the archives to Memorial Society researchers and politicians active in the truth-finding campaign of the time. The new openness existed only in Moscow, and even there it was short-lived; soon the KGB and the military managed to persuade President Yeltsin that national security was threatened by indiscriminate declassification of KGB and Communist Party archives.

Since early 1992 the right of access to government information on vital issues, though enshrined in the 1993 Constitution, has been denied repeatedly to the public. People again are losing their concern for preserving their own history. Many of them, active or passive participants in the crimes of the Soviet period, cannot admit that they themselves were fooled and that they fooled others. The elites of today are no exception. Even those of the present rulers who truly want Russia to join the European family of nations do not understand the need for public appraisal of the past.

It takes great personal courage to say publicly, "I was completely wrong in my approach to this vital problem, and I did much harm to others." It takes even greater courage when the whole nation is involved in the process of reassessing the past, especially in the absence of a stable moral tradition. If we in Russia are able to solve this problem and come to terms with reality, future generations will be able to live in peace and dignity.

This issue is of the utmost importance in any discussion of the prospects for the rule of law in Russia. The things we cherish in our past determine – sometimes unconsciously – the future we are striving to create. In some new European countries, however, the appeal for a reappraisal of the past goes unheard at all levels; people shy away from it. It is a shocking experience to realize that the things you cherished for so long are dead and rotten, that they stink, that they doom your own future.

In the seventeenth century, when the Great Plague devastated many parts of England, each morning carts laden with the corpses of those who had died during the night would stop at every house in London, and the drivers would chant, "Bring out your dead! Bring out your dead!" This is the meaning of our appeal: Let us bring out our dead!

At the same time, however, we know only too well that many of our compatriots are not prepared to realize the mortal danger of the plague of moral deafness. They still cling to putrefying images and ideas. Illusions about their recent past are like a blanket protecting them against the cold winds of change. They vote for the Communists, for Zhirinovskii, for anyone who promises to surround them again with their protective illusions. This may be a banal explanation, but the selectiveness of memory is one of the most banal phenomena in the world.

Respect for the rule of law is, so to speak, genetically coded. It is built on the experience of past generations, experience duly recorded and carefully preserved. The cultivation of a tradition takes a long time. Why did so many people in the West and, to a lesser extent, in Russia itself expect to witness the quick, triumphant progress of the rule of law in the kind of country I have described? The answers to this question center on two assertions: "It worked in Germany; it will work here" and "The free market will take care of all the rest." Such responses reflect an attempt to find direct analogies between the events in Russia and the period of transition to the rule of law in one of the leading Western democracies of today. To what extent is this attempt justifiable?

In 1996 I attended a conference in Estonia, where about 40 percent of the population are non-Estonians, mostly ethnic Russians. The subject of the conference was "integration through reconciliation." Gradually we came to confront the main problem: Is reconciliation possible at all in the post-Soviet-empire world? Reconciliation entails forgiveness, but how can forgiveness occur without repentance? To be able to repent means to be able to reappraise the past.

When I took the floor at the conference, I told the participants about my experience in Germany. I told them about the nongovernment organization (NGO) known as *Sühnezeichen-Aktion* (the Sign of Atonement Project), whose members, mostly young people, volunteer to work in the countries where German soldiers set foot during World War II and in Israel. They build and operate hospitals, educational centers, and memorial complexes. When I saw how many young Germans, half a century after the war, are ready to work without material reward to atone for the sins of their grandfathers and great-grandfathers, I felt admiration and, simultaneously, deep bitterness. Admiration, because I realized that despite twelve years of Nazi rule, the German people had managed to remain morally sound, and that the antimilitaristic views of most Germans today are based firmly on moral grounds. Bitterness, because I knew that my own people are in no way ready to atone to the people they wronged, to offer sincere apologies to nations crushed by a Soviet Army boot.

It is not that the notion of reconciliation is altogether alien to Russians. In the early 1990s this concept seemed within our grasp. On November 11, 1992, President Boris Yeltsin visited Hungary and delivered to the Hungarian Parliament a formal address that was, in my opinion, the most brilliant speech of his career. Admitting that the main threat to security and stability in Europe stemmed from some of the former Communist countries, he expressed his conviction that there would be no retreat from the strategic course of political and economic reform. He left no doubt as to Russia's desire to enter the European Community. Finally, for the first time in our history, a Russian leader stated the need to activate such an effective tool for progress as the forum of conscience, repentance, and forgiveness. It was a political program for the future, as envisaged by the president and the government.

Back home, however, Yeltsin was confronted with fierce opposition to this program in Parliament, where proponents of "a different Russian way" entailing renewed isolation from the West once again were gaining the upper hand. The deputies refused to ratify the treaty of friendship with Hungary, which the president had signed, and they vehemently attacked all the points of the proposed program. They were joined by some of the people closest to the president. The resistance was so strong that Yeltsin crumpled under it and stepped back from his program. His capitulation signaled the return to a Soviet-style "besieged fortress" psychology and the beginning of concomitant negative changes in Russian domestic and foreign policy. These changes put an end to meaningful reform and, three years later, led Russia into the criminal Chechen war.

It is never too late to repent, however, and reconciliation is still possible, though it will not come about tomorrow. Bad habits die hard, and the instinct to form a chauvinistic empire will be the last to die, I fear. Unlike the Nazi regime, the Soviet empire did not suffer total defeat in a war. Such a war would have been a nuclear nightmare for all of us. The Soviet regime simply lived out its days and collapsed. Thankfully, the collapse was the result of an evolution, not a revolution; no large-scale bloodshed accompanied it. But then let us not expect a sudden moral resurgence in people excluded from the European tradition for over seven decades. Unlike postwar Germany, Russia saw no introduction of strict new political and moral guidelines. It will take decades, perhaps generations, of reeducation, and it will require moral leadership of a kind not yet present. Moses led his people through the wilderness for forty years, until the process of their rehabilitation was complete. Let us hope that less time will be necessary for the people of post-Soviet Russia.

The Russian Orthodox Church is of no help here. In recent years it has torpedoed all the efforts of other confessions to stimulate an ecumenical movement in the country, stalled all European initiatives to that effect. The clergy was purged so thoroughly during the Soviet Dark Ages that very few Orthodox hierarchs today share what we call common values. On the contrary, they preach isolationism, and that encourages many priests to join right-wing extremist movements. It is a sad paradox that principles of remorse and forgiveness, deeply rooted in the Christian view of life, are rejected by one of the largest branches of Christendom. Russian Orthodox hierarchs contributed substantially to the adoption of a new repressive law that differentiates the "traditional" confessions from all others and treats them differently.

Bad habits truly die hard. Moreover, if left alone, they mutate and assume logically perfect final forms. In 1992 I was stunned when I first saw a banner with the hammer and sickle waving in the wind alongside a flag bearing the Nazi swastika. I knew the two were close cousins, but I had never expected that relationship to be so brazenly demonstrated in Russia, which lost many millions of its citizens in the fight against the Nazis. By 1993 this bizarre juxtaposition had become a common sight.

A political union between Communists and neo-Nazis looms large on the Russian political horizon today. Communist leaders in Parliament no longer find it necessary to hide their xenophobic sentiments. In October 1998, General Albert Makashov twice, at public rallies, vowed to kill Jews with his own hands. On December 14, 1998, Viktor Il'iukhin, chairman of the parliamentary committee on security and one of the key members of the Communist faction in Parliament, declared that "the genocide of the Russian people executed by the present regime would not have been so massive if it were not for the fact that the people around the president and in the government were mostly of Jewish nationality." On December 16, Il'iukhin insisted during a parliamentary session that what he had said about the Jews two days before was "just the truth."

Sixty years ago Nazi ideologists announced that the Jews had misappropriated all German money after World War I, created an economic crisis, and thus doomed the German people to misery. Further, the Jews were accused of the "genocide of the German people," the same assertion Communist Il'iukhin is making today. Despite the Nuremberg trials, the Nazi ideologists have won.

True, in the past several months the government has demonstrated its growing anxiety about the upsurge of right-wing and left-wing extremists and the possible political consequences of this phenomenon. The Prosecutor General's office now is trying to reactivate the dormant Article 282 of the Criminal Code and to indict those guilty of instigating racial hatred. Unfortunately, several previous moves in that direction proved to be merely short-lived campaigns aimed at bolstering the image of the government.

As for the free market – well, it is indeed free in Russia: free of any rules of the game. A populist Parliament, led by Communist and pro-Zhirinovskii factions, has blocked the laws that would permit the introduction of such rules. There are no effective laws regulating taxation, land ownership, and investment, no laws that can curb the appetites of monopolies. The banking sphere is a disaster. The biggest Russian banks play the role of moneychangers in ancient Egypt, nothing more.

The reforms instituted in 1992 were aimed first and foremost at breaking the backbone of the most ineffective economic system known: the system that is totally controlled by the state. In the next stage, reformers tried to introduce the institutions that had paid their way in the West. But again, in the absence of European tradition, their efforts to create uniform rules like those in Poland and other countries west of Russia were doomed.

Since the early 1990s the international financial community has acted according to the belief that helping Russia to introduce external evidence of a real market would suffice to start one functioning.

They never expected that the old slogan "grab what you can today, and the hell with tomorrow" would survive, even prevail, despite all the changes. Billion-dollar investments went not into industry, but into the overcentralized financial sphere. Instead of developing the real economic sector, these investments helped to enrich international and Russian speculators and actually discredited the very idea of free enterprise. They helped Moscow to build up a regional financial empire that controls all movements of capital throughout the country. Moreover, the indiscriminate transfer of Western money – not conditioned by any system of civil control, not firmly assigned to concrete projects – to post-Soviet Russia has stimulated rampant corruption at all levels of government.

The conditions for transition from totalitarian rule to the rule of law in Russia differ drastically from both those in postwar Germany and those in postwar Japan, where the absence of a rule-of-law tradition was compensated by the ten-year presence of the American army of occupation. Are we fighting for a lost cause?

Definitely not. The present situation in Russia is highly dynamic; development in any direction is possible. Tens of thousands of active NGOs, the foundation bricks of civil society, are consistently forcing administrators to follow the law and legislators to improve it. Sometimes they lose, sometimes they win; it is a daily battle. Every year, though, their presence is more noticeable. The government, in turn, has been sufficiently incorporated into the international ruling elite to wish to remain there. That implies striving for at least a minimal degree of stability, with no sudden about-faces. Of course, future developments hinge on the choice of the next president.

As for the former president – on the one hand, in the early 1990s Boris Yeltsin burned all his bridges to communism. He would be the first to be hanged if his former comrades should prove successful. On the other hand, he was unable to part with the old Soviet style of governing; his rule was opaque, authoritarian, and overly impulsive. This inevitable contradiction marred his presidency and finally ruined it. But Yeltsin must be given credit for being consistent enough in at least one respect: all those years, he doggedly pur-

sued a policy of joining international political and economic institutions. Several times Russia tried to enter the Council of Europe,
and each time it was refused because of its human rights record.
Finally, in February 1996, Strasbourg succumbed, on the condition
that Russia bring its legislation and its law-enforcement practices
into conformity with the council's binding documents in the field
of human rights.

Russian membership in the Council of Europe has given us a
powerful weapon in the struggle for the rule of law and our fundamental liberties. Even the Communist leaders no longer wish to
leave Strasbourg. There is an intense internal conflict in the Communist Party between hard-core isolationists and those who reckon
that international recognition will further their political ambitions.
I was a witness to the ritual dances of Gennadii Ziuganov, the num-
ber-one man in the party leadership, in the Parliamentary Assembly of the Council of Europe in 1996. He proclaimed that he could
not imagine Russia out of the Council and the Council without Russia. This talk was purely for outside consumption, of course – at
home he promptly went back to his usual anti-Western rhetoric –
but it helps cast light on the political process in modern Russia.

On a daily basis we resort to the legal weapons provided to us by
the Council of Europe, while campaigning for the observance of
international agreements on human rights. We campaign all the
harder because these agreements, according to Article 15 of the
Russian Constitution, have become part and parcel of our national
legislation. Council of Europe documents and Russian legislation
forbid the classification of information on vital issues, such as the
state of the environment, and guarantee citizens the right of access
to such information, for example. You may know the case of Aleksandr Nikitin, a former naval officer who turned ecologist and took
part in compiling the report on the dangers of the piled-up, un-
processed radioactive waste that Russia's Northern Fleet has been
leaving in its wake for decades. The report was sponsored by Bellona,
a Norwegian environmental foundation, which employed Nikitin as
an expert in 1994. In February 1996, when the report was finished

but not yet released, Nikitin was arrested by the FSB (Federal Security Service) and charged with espionage and revealing state secrets.

I never would have risked my personal reputation or that of my NGO by plunging headlong into Nikitin's defense if I had had any doubts about his integrity. We conducted an investigation of our own and concluded that Nikitin had never been a spy, that the case was politically motivated from the outset. We saw Nikitin's arrest as an attempt by certain political forces to obstruct broad participation by Russia in international cooperation, to isolate the country anew from the civilized world. We realized that, should Nikitin be pronounced guilty on the basis of the ludicrous evidence presented by the FSB, any Russian citizen who had ever collaborated with any foreign organization or foundation would be threatened with political repression.

In June 1996, we formed a committee, of which I am the chairman, in defense of Aleksandr Nikitin. Together with other reputable human rights NGOs, we started an intensive campaign at home and abroad. Bellona continued its support for Nikitin and left no stone unturned in its effort to explain to the world what he had done for the good of humanity. Together with Bellona representatives, I gave evidence to the Legal and Human Rights Committee of the Council of Europe's Parliamentary Assembly in Strasbourg. That committee appointed a special rapporteur on the Nikitin case. It was the approaching visit of this rapporteur in January 1997 that led in December 1996 to Nikitin's release pending trial. For the first time the FSB, against its will, was forced to release from prison a man it had officially charged.

In October 1998, Nikitin's case was brought before the court at last, but after five days of hearings the judge returned the case to the FSB prosecutors because of the "inconclusive results of expert examination." He did not dare to pronounce a verdict of "not guilty"; the FSB is still a mighty agency. Had Nikitin been acquitted, it would have meant that for more than three years the FSB had been wasting taxpayers' money in pursuit of its own interests, to the detriment of national security. Heads may roll, since the case is well-known worldwide, and the FSB needed a verdict of guilty. It was a clear defeat for the security service; however, for the first time a Russian court openly defied the FSB. Small victories like this one may eventually culminate in the triumph of the rule of law.

We now realize that some decline in the vigor of the reforms was inevitable. To succeed, economic reforms should be accompanied by a parallel process of reeducation on a mass scale, starting at the grass-roots level. Despite all other urgent needs, a significant portion of the foreign loans should have been directed toward that end. Efforts in this direction were minimal, however. No rule of law can be introduced successfully without new, long-term educational programs. Russians have never been a law-abiding people, and the Communists aggravated the situation to an extreme. The law was so ruthless to the man in the street that striving to cheat the authorities, to break established rules, and to "beat the system" became a kind of national sport. We now face decades of unswerving hard work to reeducate the Russian people, restore their historic memory, awaken their capacity for atonement, help them find new moral guidelines, and involve as many of them as possible in the process of building a developed, civil society. The work we are doing today will benefit our grandchildren: God forbid that they should have to start everything anew.

RUSSIA'S TRANSITION TO DEMOCRACY

CONSTITUTIONAL JUSTICE AND

THE PROTECTION OF CIVIL LIBERTIES

MARAT SALIKOV

Marat Salikov is a professor of constitutional law at the Ural State Law Academy in Ekaterinburg. A distinguished legal scholar with more than sixty academic publications to his credit, he also wrote the first casebook for the teaching of constitutional law in post-Soviet Russia. Professor Salikov recently was awarded a doctoral degree by, and has been a visiting professor at, St. Louis University Law School.

Introduction

THE TRANSITION from authoritarianism to a civil society ruled by law is seldom easy. The transition now under way in Russia is particularly painful. The goals of the transition were – and still are – political democratization, economic reform, cooperative partnership with the West, and the guarantee of civil liberties.

Rights, liberties, and their protection are an extremely important indication of the level of development of a civil society and its ability to withstand the state's tendencies to encroach upon those freedoms. Formerly there existed in Russia a legislative barrier that obstructed the exercise of some rights and liberties which, although set forth in the Constitution, could not be enjoyed because direct application of the provisions was impossible. Moreover, even if there had been no such barrier, the existing state regime would not have allowed these rights and liberties to be exercised fully, because they contradicted the underlying political principles of the regime.

Contemporary Russia is moving slowly toward freedom, and this progress is evident both in the establishment of totally new public institutions – such as the division of powers, constitutional review, alternative elections, and the multiparty system – and in the giving of real strength to institutions that existed on paper but were not operative in reality; for example, the exercise of civil liberties that were set forth in the Constitution.

This chapter analyzes the historical development of the rights and liberties provided in the Constitution and their protection by the court system. Here we are not talking about courts of general jurisdiction, but instead the Constitutional Court, whose duty it is to ensure protection of fundamental rights. The Constitutional Court stands apart from the general courts, because its tasks are specific. It does not try criminal, civil, and other cases on their merits. Rather, as a body of constitutional review, the Court deals with the constitutionality of statutes. This process gives individuals a greater prospect that their civil liberties will be protected, because the Constitutional Court's work reduces the number of unconstitutional statutes and, as a result, the potential for violation of civil liberties. The ultimate goal is the construction of a constitutionally governed society in Russia.

Constitutional Regulation of Rights and Liberties: The Historical Background

In the second half of the nineteenth century a gradual process changing the form of government from an absolute monarchy to a constitutional one took hold in Russia. This process was neither smooth nor rapid. On the contrary, it ran counter to the interests of the monarchy and was accompanied by the growth of a revolutionary movement. In this regard, the tsar's decree "On the Improvement of Public Order," dated October 17, 1905 – often called the first Russian Constitution – was incredibly important from the standpoint of the development of protections for human rights. This document proclaimed such rights and freedoms as respect for the inviolability of the person, freedom of religion, freedom of expression (censorship was abolished), freedom of assembly, and freedom of association, including the right to form and join political parties and trade unions. Of course the decree was somewhat limited, yet it was the first edict in Russian history to deal with civil and political liberties. After the armed uprising of autumn 1905 was suppressed, a new decree was issued: "On Changing the Election Regulations of the State Duma." This document attracted broad masses of the population to take part in the election process. Yet the elections themselves were not direct, nor did they offer the same rights to the different groups of the electorate. During the same period, the peasants' rights were expanded. Restrictions on their choice of residence were eased, for example, and they no longer were required to reside in the place where they were registered, but could live where they worked or had property.

In February 1917, the Russian monarchy was overthrown. While the Provisional Government was in charge, some innovations were introduced in the regulation of rights and liberties. Capital punishment was abolished, although it was later reinstated for the military. The powers of local governments were broadened. Attempts were made to remove restrictions on social, religious, and national practices. The activity of the Provisional Government, however, was complicated by political, economic, and social crises. In addition, Russia was still involved in World War I. For these reasons, the reforms were halfhearted, and not only where rights and freedoms were concerned.

The October Revolution interrupted Russia's movement toward the creation of a republic along European or American lines, where rights and liberties are not only set forth constitutionally, but also guaranteed by the state and a well-run judicial system. It is interesting to scrutinize the constitutional regulation of rights and freedoms in Russia after the Bolsheviks' rise to power, in comparison with both previous legal regulation and regulation in subsequent constitutions. Prior to 1993 there were four Russian constitutions, adopted in 1918, 1925, 1937, and 1978, respectively.[1]

The Constitution of 1918 was Russia's first written constitution and also the most ideological. It erased almost all the gains of the previous period. The state was no longer obliged to guarantee individual rights and liberties or to refrain from interfering in private lives and freedoms. As Lenin wrote, "We don't recognize anything 'private'." The state could control everything, without leaving the slightest degree of independence from the bureaucratic state machinery to members of society. Such institutions and principles as parliamentary democracy, responsible government, the separation of powers, the right of opposition, and the rule of law were forgotten and canceled because the new government professed a "new" ideology. Executive power, which had grown very strong in the absence of judicial control, denied individual rights and freedoms altogether. Many social groups were deprived of electoral rights, among them, people who used hired labor, people who lived on interest income, private merchants, priests, white-collar workers, and agents of the former police force. Even the classes that formed the "workers' and peasants' state" were unequal under the constitution: workers were represented in the representative bodies (soviets) in greater numbers than peasants. Political parties were banned, and their leaders were imprisoned or shot. One peculiarity of the 1918 Constitution deserves special mention: it was the only constitution that recognized violence as a tool for establishing the principles of the new socialist state. Article 3 of this document mentioned "abolishing the parasitic strata of society," "mercilessly suppressing exploiters," "violently abolishing private property," and "compulsory confiscation of property without remuneration."

1. After the Soviet Union was established in 1922, the constituent republics, including Russia, issued their own constitutions, which could not contradict the national constitution. The Russian Federation's constitutions of 1925, 1937, and 1978, therefore, necessarily repealed almost all the provisions of the corresponding Soviet constitutions of 1924, 1936, and 1977.

The second Russian constitution was issued in 1925, following the Soviet Constitution of 1924. The chief reason for adopting a new constitution was the need to sanction the formation of a new state – the Soviet Union – and to regulate the division of powers between the federal government and the constituent republics of the state. The new document contained very few articles concerning the legal regulation of rights and freedoms. It used the previous constitution as a model, yet it considerably softened provisions concerning violence and the need for abolishing or suppressing parasitic elements of society.

Adoption of the Soviet Constitution of 1936, often referred to as the Stalin Constitution, resulted in adoption of the Russian Constitution of 1937. The need for these documents arose out of the attainment of a new stage in the development of the state ("building the fundamentals of socialism") and the completion of the process of liquidating the exploitive classes and elements of society.

In analyzing the constitutions of the 1930s and their implementation, one must consider two characteristics. On the one hand, many rights and liberties not included in previous constitutions – personal inviolability, freedom of residence, the right to private correspondence, the right to work, and the freedoms of speech, religion, assembly, association, and the press – were set down. The procedure for deprivation of political rights was annulled. For the first time, universal, direct, and equal elections by secret ballot were envisaged. Equality of rights for all citizens was proclaimed. On the other hand, observance of the rights and liberties mentioned above was either incomplete or totally impossible. For example, in elections people could vote only for those listed on the ballot; there were no write-in candidates. Equality of rights for all citizens was acknowledged regardless of "nationality and race," but there was room for discrimination on other grounds. Exercising political rights was possible only in accordance with the "interests of the workers and for the purpose of strengthening the socialist order." The church was completely controlled by state bodies, so that freedom of religion could hardly become a reality. Suppression of individual rights and liberties was a purposeful policy of the authoritarian regime, as the following facts illustrate: the annihilation and eviction of millions of peasants, which was justified by the "struggle with kulak exploiters"; the elimination of the freedoms of speech, press, and assembly, justified by the "struggle" against "counterrevolutionary agitation and propaganda"; and the forced deportation of entire ethnic groups, justified by the "struggle against collaboration" and "counterrevolutionary elements." The creation of an obligatory passport system and compulsory registration of the urban population were obstacles to the peasants' right to move and to choose their places of residence. Free exit from the country and marriage to foreigners were also prohibited. Although changes after Stalin's death softened the regime somewhat, its basic nature did not change at all.

In 1978 the fourth Russian constitution was adopted, in accordance with the Soviet Constitution of 1977 (the Brezhnev constitution). This was the last socialist effort to reconcile a constitutional proclamation of expanded civil rights and liberties with the antidemocratic nature of the regime. For example, the constitution recognized the principle of equal rights for citizens regardless of birth, social origin, property, sex, nationality, education, language, religion, place of residence, and other circumstances. It articulated such new rights as the right to housing and health care. Under the constitution, the most important matters of public life were based on referendum and public discussion. At that time, several important international treaties dealing with human rights were ratified and came into force. But the constitution itself was essentially a declaration of political policy and aims, not a directly binding governing document. It was not even really a law, since a law should work, and the constitution did not work. It was no more than a manifesto. The exercise of political rights was possible only in accordance with the aims of "constructing socialism."

Extremely important changes took place when Russia began to move toward democratization during the period from 1989 to 1993. The first step in this process was the holding of alternative parliamentary elections, a tremendous achievement for the country. A new legislative body was formed in 1989 on an alternative basis. Then, in the following four years, numerous amendments (some scholars counted about five hundred) were made to the Constitution. Among the most important were those abolishing the one-party system and establishing a multiparty system, proclaiming the doctrine of separation of powers, instituting judicial control and creating the Constitutional Court, recognizing the right to private property, and instituting the office of the presidency. On November 22, 1991, the Declaration of Rights and Freedoms of Man and of the Citizen was issued, and it later was included in the Constitution. Such administrative divisions as *krais, oblasts,* and cities of federal significance (Moscow and St. Petersburg) were recognized as members of the Federation upon signing the Federal Treaty on March 31, 1992. Before that time, only the republics, the autonomous *okrugs,* and the autonomous *oblasts* were considered members of the Federation. Although the newly included territories were not given powers equal to those of republics (the position of the autonomies, with extremely limited powers in comparison with the other members, was even worse), the very fact of their recognition was a big step toward the creation of true federalism in Russia.

In 1993 the new Russian Constitution was adopted. The manner of its adoption – through an all-Russian referendum – was evidence of important changes, not only in the people's minds, but also in the protection of human rights and freedoms. According to the Constitution, rights and liberties have the same force of law as the Constitution itself. If we analyze the second chapter of the Constitution, where rights and freedoms are enumerated, we see that they are much the same as those found in the major international instruments addressing human rights and freedoms, such as the Universal Declaration of Human Rights, the International Covenant of Civil and Political Rights, and the European Convention on the Protection of Human Rights and Fundamental Freedoms.

Parenthetically, Russia has signed and ratified all those documents and therefore recognizes international and regional protections for human rights. After the Constitution was published and became effective, Parliament passed many additional laws in this area. Among these were the laws "On the Referendum of the Russian Federation," "On the Human Rights Ombudsman of the Russian Federation," "On the Judicial System of the Russian Federation," "On the Procedure of Departure from and Entry into the Russian Federation," "On Basic Guarantees of Voting Rights and the Right to Referendum of Citizens of the Russian Federation," and "On Public Association." Even earlier, the laws "On the Right of Citizens of the Russian Federation to Freedom of Movement, Choice of Place of Residence and Domicile within the Borders of the Russian Federation," and "On Appealing to the Court Concerning Actions in Violation of Citizens' Rights and Freedoms" were passed. Work on additional laws dealing with the exercise of particular rights and freedoms is under way in Russia today.

Such laws are indeed important, yet, because violations of rights and liberties in our country still occur, the work of all Russian courts, regardless of their jurisdiction, is very significant. Looking at a comparatively new type of court for Russia – the Constitutional Court – one must say that it deals with the protection of rights and liberties in a special manner. As mentioned above, the Constitutional Court does not hear criminal, civil, and other cases on their merits. Rather, it deals with the constitutionality of legislative and other statutes. In my opinion, this task is much more difficult than that of a court of general jurisdiction and has more important juridical consequences. Let us consider the protection of rights and liberties by means of constitutional justice, which was practically unknown to the Russian judicial system until recently.

Russian Constitutional Justice: The Initial Experience

The creation of the Constitutional Court in October 1991 signified a radical change, not only for the institution of judicial protection but also for Russia's machinery of government as a whole. On the one hand, the judicial system gained a specialized body of constitutional control and, on the other hand, judicial power influenced the separation of powers. An important counterbalance to legislative and executive power came into being. In accordance with the constitution in effect at that time and the law "On the Constitutional Court," passed on July 12, 1992, the Constitutional Court was proclaimed to be the highest judicial authority dealing with the protection of the constitutional system and was granted broad powers. In particular, the Court was authorized to exercise its judicial power by hearing cases on the constitutionality of international treaties, statutes, presidential decrees, and governmental regulations; the activity of political parties and other public associations; law enforcement procedures; the settling of disputes about the jurisdiction of various state entities; and the rendering of decisions in instances prescribed by law.

Between 1992 and 1993 the Constitutional Court considered a number of cases involving citizens' complaints and held unconstitutional the following actions: firing an individual on the basis of age, found to be illegal discrimination; imposing discriminatory penalties upon workers in the prosecutor's office; evicting an individual from unlawfully occupied accommodations with a prosecutor's sanction, without the right to lodge a complaint against the sanction, found to be a restriction of the right to judicial and other protection; limiting reimbursement for damages to a specified time of payment on reinstatement of an unlawfully dismissed individual. The Constitutional Court confirmed the principle of equality in contractual relations between the state and a citizen. It acknowledged the constitutionality of citizens' demands for the state to discharge its obligations with respect to special-purpose checks for the purchase of cars, as well as the indexation of citizens' income and savings. The Constitutional Court's attitude toward the protection of the rights of association, free speech, freedom of the press, and the right to vote may also be considered an achievement.

In considering cases involving individual complaints by Russian citizens, foreigners, and stateless persons, the Court found unconstitutional certain practices based upon statutory provisions but not the corresponding provisions. The latter could be repealed only by the bodies that had passed them. The Court's action caused it considerable difficulty. For example, the Court's decision of January 27, 1993, found unconstitutional the rule requiring a time limit on payment for absence from work when a person was unlawfully dismissed. This rule was based on the provisions of Part 2, Article 213 of the Labor Code of the Russian Federation. However, in a ruling of June 15, 1995, the Court acknowledged that courts should, as before, confine themselves to collecting compensation for one year as envisaged by the given rule, because the Russian Parliament had not amended the Labor Code correspondingly.

The first stage of the development of constitutional control in the Russian Federation was not devoid of mistakes and extremes. This result may be partially explained by "growing pains." Constitutional control, which has a long tradition in Western democracies, is practically a novel concept for Russia, apart from the brief experience of the work done by the USSR Committee on Constitutional Supervision.[2] The Constitutional Court found itself at the center of the conflict between the legislative and the executive powers, and it failed to take an independent and impartial stand. It was drawn into political confrontation and often exceeded its jurisdiction. A number of judges did not agree with the Court's position overall and refused to participate in its work until the new Parliament of the Russian Federation – the Federal Assembly – began to function. In these circumstances, any decisions not reached by a plurality of the Court would be invalid. For this reason, on October 5, 1993, the Constitutional Court relinquished its duty to weigh the constitutionality of statutes and treaties. The Court resumed its activity (with new members) only after the Constitution of the Russian Federation of December 12, 1993, and the federal constitutional law "On the Constitutional Court of the Russian Federation" of June 24, 1994, were passed.

2. The first specialized body of constitutional oversight was the USSR's Committee on Constitutional Supervision, founded in April 1990 in accordance with the law "On Constitutional Supervision in the USSR."

The Constitutional Court as a Tool for the Protection of Rights and Liberties

With the beginning of the Constitutional Court's activity under the new federal constitutional law, the number of cases involving citizens' rights and liberties increased considerably. The broadening range of the Court's activity in this sphere (from the assessment of the constitutionality of regulations to the assessment of the underlying statute) serves as an additional guarantee of fundamental rights and freedoms.

It should be noted that the Court defends the rights and freedoms of citizens not only in cases of direct complaint and court inquiries as Part 4, Article 125 of the Constitution requires, but also in cases involving the constitutionality of statutes and treaties. For example, the Court's ruling of January 18, 1996, in a case involving a number of provisions of the Altai Krai Charter, found unconstitutional an article of the Charter that contemplated the election of the executive power by a body of representatives. The Court recognized that this article violated electoral rights. In a ruling of April 4, 1996, concerning a number of statutes of Russian Federation members regulating citizens' registration, the Court found violations of the civil right to freedom of movement and choice of residence. The Court also noted the violation of this right when trying the "Chechen case." It should be noted that in these decisions, state entities rather than citizens appealed to the Court. The Court considers cases fully and thoroughly, not only analyzing disputed provisions from the point of view of constitutionality, but also examining possible violations of, or restrictions on, fundamental rights and freedoms.

The cases of the Constitutional Court involving the protection of civil rights and freedoms can be divided into the following groups: cases involving the rules of criminal statutes and criminal procedure; cases involving administrative law and limiting the rights of private property owners; cases involving violations of labor and social rights and freedoms; and cases involving the restriction of freedom of residence. In addition, the Court has entertained cases involving inheritance, Russian citizenship, and the legal status of stateless people.

Constitutional Review of the Rules
of Criminal Law and Criminal Procedure

The Court's rulings on criminal procedure have upheld the right of relief (provisions of May 3 and November 13, 1995; February 2 and June 13, 1996) and found unconstitutional a number of provisions of the Code of Criminal Procedure. In a case involving complaints by K. M. Kul'nev, Yu. V. Lukashov, and I. P. Serebrennikov, the possibility of a review process was analyzed and decisions were rendered by the highest judicial supervisory authority: the Presidium of the Supreme Court of the Russian Federation. In a ruling of February 2, 1996, the Court concluded that the provisions of the Code of Criminal Procedure establishing ultimate judicial supervisory powers are constitutional only when the restrictions envisaged do not preclude the possibility of other procedural remedies for judicial error. In particular, the Court considered the possibility of Russian citizens' application to international bodies for protection of human rights and freedoms, as well as the possibility of repeated consideration by means of the procedure for reopening a case. In view of its conclusion, the Court found that the provision of the Code of Criminal Procedure restricting the grounds for reopening a case was unconstitutional.

Another case examined by the Constitutional Court, involving the complaint of V. V. Shchelukhin, is of interest from the point of view of both civil rights protection and procedural rights. In its decision, the Court found unconstitutional a provision of the Code of Criminal Procedure contemplating suspension of the time limits for investigation and custody during the period when the defendant prepares his defense. At the same time, the Court noted that the rule "loses its force" six months after a ruling and postponed the execution of a decision. Justice N. V. Vitruk, in dissent, noted that the Court's ruling in this regard contradicts the general principles of constitutional law and the law "On the Constitutional Court," according to Article 79, Section 3 of which "acts or separate provisions found unconstitutional lose their force." In the justice's opinion the Court, having found the rule to be unconstitutional, could not acknowledge its operation within a period of six months. However, it does not appear that the Court exceeded the limits of the law, because Article 79, Section 3 does not establish definite time limits for loss of force of statutes or separate provisions that are found unconstitutional. In addition, Article 80 provides for the Court's right to establish time limits for execution of a judgment independently.

The case of citizen V. A. Smirnov is interesting because contradictions between public and private interests are clearly revealed. On the one hand, there are the state's efforts to protect itself and its interests; on the other, there are efforts to protect individual rights guaranteed by the Constitution. In the matter at issue, the claimant contested the Criminal Code's provisions concerning treason in the form of betraying state or military secrets to a foreign state, taking flight to a foreign country or refusing to return from abroad, and rendering aid to a foreign government in the conduct of a hostile action. The provisions regarding flight to a foreign country and refusal to return were found unconstitutional, because the Constitution guarantees the right of foreign travel and freedom of return. The Court held that such actions cannot encroach upon the state's defense, sovereignty, territorial integrity, security, and defense capability. Accordingly, the new Criminal Code does not contain those provisions.

The Court heard issues involving the possible institution of criminal proceedings against judges when disagreement is expressed by an appropriate board of expert judges, on the basis of complaints by R. I. Mukhametshin and A. I. Barbash. The Court's ruling of May 7, 1996, states that the provisions of the law "On the Status of Judges" cannot be interpreted as precluding the possibility of an appeal from the decision of the board of expert judges, because the statutory procedure is a means of ensuring judicial independence. Therefore, the refusal of the board of expert judges to institute criminal proceedings against a judge "is not an insuperable obstacle" to an appeal. This decision by the board may be appealed first to the Supreme Collegium of Expert Judges of the Russian Federation, and then to a court, according to the law "On Appealing to the Court Regarding Actions That Violate Citizens' Rights and Freedoms," as the decision affects the rights of both the judge and the aggrieved citizen.

The Court has consistently affirmed constitutionally guaranteed rights and liberties, as demonstrated in a case involving the provisions of the Russian Federation's law "On State Secrets." The case arose out of a number of citizens' complaints. The court of general jurisdiction refused to allow an attorney without access to state secrets to participate in a trial. In its decision of March 27, 1996, the Court ruled that barring attorneys from participation in a trial by reason of their lack of access to state secrets violated the Constitution of the Russian Federation and its provisions for every person to receive qualified legal assistance at every stage of a criminal proceeding.

In its ruling of November 3, 1995, the Court found unconstitutional Article 209, Section 5 of the Code of Criminal Procedure, which limits the possibility of an appeal from the rules governing dismissal of a criminal case. The rule of the Code of Criminal Procedure discussed above was mentioned by the Court in another ruling a year later, on October 28, 1996, in a case involving Article 6 of the Code of Criminal Procedure. Complainant O. V. Sushkov asked the court to find the article unconstitutional because, in his opinion, it "violated the constitutional principle of presumption of innocence and did not entitle the accused to object to the dismissal of a case and demand that it be tried on its merits." Having noted that criminal procedural legislation no longer contains a direct prohibition on appeal of a dismissed criminal case, because the ruling of November 13, 1995, removed the obstacle previous to an appeal, the Court found Article 6 of the Code of Criminal Procedure unconstitutional, because "the dismissal of a criminal case owing to a change in circumstances does not establish a person's guilt in the crime committed, does not prevent him from exercising his right to defense, and presupposes his agreement to dismiss the criminal case on the stated grounds."

In its ruling of November 28, 1996, the Constitutional Court again examined the constitutionality of the provisions of the Code of Criminal Procedure. This time the Court examined Article 418 of the Code in response to an inquiry of the Karatuzskii Raion Court of Krasnoiarskii Krai. The lower court had found unlawful the combination in one case of the institution of criminal proceedings, a statement of charge, and sentencing. Article 418 applies to criminal proceedings in which pretrial preparation takes the form of a report; that is, when a body of inquest, without having instituted criminal proceedings, collects materials confirming the commission of a crime, draws up a report concerning the circumstances of the crime, and directs it to a court with the prosecutor's approval. The court, in accordance with Article 418 of the Code of Criminal Procedure, makes a decision to begin a criminal proceeding, states the charge, identifies a specific article of criminal law under which the accused is called to account, and then, in accordance with Article 419 of the Code of Criminal Procedure, decides the case. The Constitutional Court concluded, after a thoroughgoing appraisal, that the Code's provisions "empowering a judge to institute criminal proceedings on the basis of materials prepared in a report or to refuse to institute them" and envisaging "the judge's duty to state a charge in the decision of instituting criminal proceedings" are unconstitutional. The Court explained that the administration of justice is the exclusive function of the judiciary, and thus a court cannot perform any functions not in accordance with its position as a body of justice. Exercise of such powers as initiating a prosecution and maintaining a prosecution must be entrusted to special agencies, that is, pretrial bodies of inquest, pretrial investigation, and the prosecutor's office. "The court must examine the results of their activities, objectively and impartially deciding questions of lawfulness and grounds for bringing an accusation, as well as considering complaints against the actions and decisions of the officials conducting judicial proceedings in the pretrial stages."

As previously noted, the ruling held unconstitutional the provision giving a court the function of stating a charge. The Constitutional Court noted that this procedure makes it difficult for a judge who has instituted criminal proceedings and stated a charge against a particular individual to give an objective analysis and legal assessment of the circumstances of the case, because acquittal or other judgment in favor of the accused may seem to demonstrate his erroneous judgment. Thus, several constitutional principles are violated: judicial oversight of the rights of citizens in criminal proceedings; the conduct of judicial proceedings on an adversarial basis; and the individual's right to have his case tried by an independent and impartial court. The ruling says that "the judge, having received a report and other accompanying materials concerning the crime and having considered them sufficient, has a right and obligation to set a date to decide only those questions which are to be decided in accordance with the general rules of the Code of Criminal Procedure."

The conflict between public interest and the interest of individual citizens was distinctly revealed in yet another decision where the Constitutional Court analyzed provisions of the Code of Criminal Procedure. A ruling of January 28, 1997, addressed the constitutionality of Article 47, Section 4 in connection with a number of individual citizens' complaints alleging violation of their constitutional rights. Under Article 47, Section 4 only attorneys and representatives of trade unions and other public associations may serve as defense counsel in criminal trials.

The Chamber of the Constitutional Court,[3] which considered the case, reached a five-four decision. The Court's plurality decision states that the constitutional "right to choose an attorney (defense counsel) independently does not mean the right to choose any person in the capacity of attorney at the defendant's discretion and does not presuppose participation of any person in the capacity of

---

3. The Federal Constitutional Court has two chambers, which include ten and nine justices, respectively.

attorney." The Court characterized the right as a manifestation of the more general right to qualified legal assistance. Because the state guarantees this right, it is entitled to establish statutorily the conditions under which a person may render such services. Accordingly, the Court upheld the provision concerning admittance of an attorney as defense counsel.

Of particular interest is the Court's recognition that a representative of a trade union or other public association may serve as defense counsel only when a corresponding report and an identification card are presented. The Court's opinion emphasizes that the law does not require that such a representative have legal training or any type of professional expertise and experience. In the Court's opinion, this "makes doubtful the possibility of ensuring the defendant the right to receive qualified legal aid." At the same time, the Court declined to consider the constitutionality of this provision of the Code because the claimants had not raised the issue.

In my opinion, the Court should have examined the appropriateness of excluding as defense counsel persons other than attorneys and representatives of public associations, even if those persons are licensed to render legal services for remuneration. As noted previously, there were four dissents. Justice V. O. Luchin, noting that Article 47, Section 4 of the Code of Criminal Procedure does not define the criteria of professionalism for legal assistance rendered to a defendant, concludes that the provision of the Code is unconstitutional because it restricts the rights of suspects and defendants to qualified legal assistance by persons who are not members of a bar association.[4] In Justice Luchin's opinion, "there are no grounds not to admit, in the capacity of defense lawyers, persons with licenses to render paid legal services officially, on behalf of the state."

Three other justices, E. M. Ametistov, V. I. Oleinik, and N. T. Vedernikov, express a similar point of view. In their dissents they

---

4. According to Justice Luchin, "This article says nothing about a defense lawyer's legal qualification or competence; it merely cites his membership in either a bar association or a public association."

point to the difference between the terms "attorney" and "defense counsel" in the text of the Constitution. The word "attorney" is narrower in the sphere of its application because it refers only to the activity of professional lawyers. The term "defense counsel" is broader because it refers to the activity of any person engaged in the defense or representation of someone's interests in court and in judicial proceedings. In addition, Justice Ametistov refers to the materials of the Constitutional Conference in support of the contention that the authors of the Constitution intended to ensure the right of persons taken into custody and charged with committing a crime to an independent and very wide choice of defense counsel, including lawyers who practice privately and who are not members of bar associations. All of the dissenting justices agree that there is a flaw in Article 47, Section 4 of the Code of Criminal Procedure insofar as it prevents nonmembers of bar associations from serving as defense counsel.

Constitutional Protection of Private Property Rights

On December 17, 1996, the Constitutional Court handed down its opinion in a case on the constitutionality of Article 11, Section 1, items 2 and 3 of the Russian Federation's law "On the Federal Tax Police Authorities." The inquiry was made by creators of limited liability partnerships and concerned the lawfulness of the collection of tax arrears by the tax police, as well as the amount of the penalties and other sanctions envisaged by legislation. In the claimants' opinion, such collection violated private property rights and contradicted Article 35 of the Constitution of the Russian Federation.[5] The Constitutional Court, having divided all the challenged sanctions into two groups, ruled that the legislative provisions govern-

5. Article 35 of the Russian Constitution, in particular, provides protection of the right of private property and the right to own property, to enjoy it, and to dispose of it both separately and jointly. In addition, the owner can be deprived of the property only by a court judgment.

34

ing one of these groups – the collection of tax arrears and fines in the case of late tax payment – do not indisputably contravene the Constitution of the Russian Federation. In contrast, those provisions governing collection of penalties as well as the entire amount of hidden or understated income (profit) without their agreement are unconstitutional. With respect to the first group of sanctions, the Court took the point of view that the right of private property is not absolute. That is, in accordance with the Constitution and numerous rules of international law, this right may be restricted by federal law under certain circumstances: when it is necessary, for example, to protect the fundamentals of the constitutional system, morality, health, and other persons' rights and lawful interests; to secure the country's defense; and to ensure the security of the state. Further, the Court analyzed the nature of the constitutional duty to pay lawfully established taxes and dues. In the Court's unanimous opinion, it is of "a specific, namely, of a public and legal (civil and legal) nature, which is due to the public nature of the state and state power. . . . Collection of taxes cannot be considered an arbitrary deprivation of the owner's property. This constitutes a lawful taking of a part of that property as a result of a constitutional public duty." The relations of tax law are based on one party's legal subordination to the other, and the tax agency's requirement and the taxpayer's duty result not from the contract but from law. Any dispute over failure to fulfill a tax obligation falls within the framework of public law (tax law in the given case). The Constitutional Court especially stressed the taxpayer's right to appeal the decisions and actions (or inactions) of tax agencies and their officials as envisaged by Article 46 of the Constitution of the Russian Federation.

With respect to the second group of sanctions, the Court took the point of view that collection of the entire amount of hidden or understated income (profit) and imposition of penalties is not within the framework of the tax obligation and is of a punitive, rather than a restorative, nature, being a punishment for tax violation. The Constitutional Court noted that a tax police agency indisputably had the right to impose penalties on a legal entity when it detected a tax violation. However, the taxpayer, in turn, has the right to appeal this judgment to a court and/or a higher tax agency. In this case, "a penalty cannot be collected irrevocably and collection must be postponed until the court has reached a decision concerning the taxpayer's claim." Otherwise, Article 35, Section 3 of the Constitution is violated since it provides that a person can be deprived of his property only by court judgment.

The Court analyzed a similar problem (protection of the right of private property) when it examined the constitutionality of the provisions of the Customs Code, Article 280 (ruling of May 20, 1997). These provisions envisage the customs authorities' right to confiscate goods and means of transportation involved in a violation of customs regulations. The Novgorod Oblast' Court tried the case of citizen A. V. Andreev, to whom that penalty had been applied, and submitted an inquiry to the Constitutional Court. In the Novgorod court's opinion, granting the customs authorities this right infringed upon the right of private property and contradicts Article 35, Section 3 of the Constitution, which, as noted above, provides that "a person can be deprived of his property only by a court judgment." Having studied the record, the Court concluded that the customs authorities' confiscation of the property as a sanction for a customs violation did not contradict the requirements of the Constitution, provided there is a guarantee of subsequent judicial review to protect the owner's rights.

Justice A. L. Kononov dissented from the Court's judgment in this case. He rejected the linking of the judicial guarantee envisaged by Article 35, Section 3 of the Constitution solely to the filing of a complaint. The justice asserted that "otherwise, a person who has not been duly informed about an administrative decision, or who has neither the opportunity nor the wish to lodge a complaint, is automatically deprived of the constitutional guarantees of protection of property." Justice Kononov drew attention to what he saw as the disparity between the Constitutional Court's holding and its other chamber's decision of December 17, 1996, in the case involving the provisions of Article 11 of the Russian Federation law "On the Federal Tax Police Authorities." The justice noted that in that decision, which involved a taxpayer's disagreement with the administrative collection of payments, as well as in a case where a penalty takes the form of civil, administrative, and criminal sanctions according to Article 35, Section 3 of the Constitution, the question may be decided only by means of trial. Because of this divergence of opinion in the Constitutional Court chambers, Justice Kononov believed that the case should be referred to the plenary session.

Constitutional Review of the Rules of Voting Legislation

In a ruling of June 21, 1996, the Constitutional Court found unconstitutional two provisions of Article 20 of the law of the Republic of Bashkortostan[6] "On Elections of Deputies to the State Assembly of the Republic of Bashkortostan" of October 13, 1994. The first provision stated that as a necessary condition for a candidate to be registered, voters' signatures from the corresponding voting district totaling not less than 5 percent of the total number of voters must be collected in his support. Emphasizing that regulation of human and civil rights and freedoms (voting rights, in this case) is ascribed by the Constitution to the powers of the Russian Federation, and their protection is ascribed to the joint competence of the Federation and its constituents, the Court referred to the federal law of December 6, 1994, "On Fundamental Guarantees of the Voting Rights of Citizens of the Russian Federation." This law states that "the maximum number of signatures necessary to register a candidate cannot exceed 2 percent of the number of voters in the corresponding voting district."

The second provision of the challenged law of Bashkortostan contemplated the following procedures for the candidate's registration: the obligatory submission, by a group of voters to the district voting commission, of the minutes (or extracts from the minutes)

---

6. Bashkortostan is one of the twenty-one republics that are members of the Russian Federation.

of a general meeting held by the voters in keeping with their places of residence, work, or study; the submission of a list, certified in accordance with established procedure, of not fewer than one hundred persons who voted for the candidate's nomination, this list containing surnames, first names, patronymics, addresses, and numbers and series of passports or other identification cards.

In contrast, the federal law establishes as the only requirements for a candidate's registration, upon his presentation by the associations and voters who have nominated him, the availability of the candidate's application containing his agreement to cast his ballot in the given voting district and the required number of voters' signatures in support of the candidate. The Constitutional Court concluded that the law of the Republic of Bashkortostan, in comparison with the federal law, had introduced additional requirements restricting the right of citizens and residents of the republic to elect and to be elected. In dissent, the Court noted that "having increased the number of voters' signatures and having complicated the procedure for their collection, the republic's law has put the citizens of Bashkortostan in an unequal position, compared with the citizens of other members of the Russian Federation, in the exercise of their voting rights." Under the Constitution, the state guarantees the equality of human and civil rights regardless of the citizen's place of residence.

Constitutional Protection of Labor, Housing, and Other Social Rights

The following rulings relate to violation of citizens' labor and social rights: a ruling of March 11, 1996 (concerning citizens who suffered exposure to radiation as a result of the Maiak production plant accident in 1957 and the disposal of radioactive waste products in the Techa River); a ruling of May 23, 1995 (concerning children whose parents were subjected to political repression, and acknowledgment of the children who were in penal institutions, exile, places of deportation, and special settlements with parents who were repressed and suffered from more than political forms of repression alone); a ruling of October 16, 1995 (concerning pensioners who were deprived of their pensions owing to suspension of payments while they were in penal institutions); a ruling of May 17, 1995 (concerning civil aviation workers' right to strike); a ruling of June 6, 1995 (concerning officers of the militia discharged on the initiative of the head of the office of internal affairs upon completion of the period of service that qualifies for the receipt of a pension).

In 1995, the Court heard two cases involving housing rights of citizens. In a ruling of April 25, 1995, involving Article 54, Sections 1 and 2 of the Housing Code of the Russian Federation in connection with L. N. Sitalova's complaint, the Court found unconstitutional a provision of the rules relying upon "the established order" as the procedure for moving into accommodations, provided that the conditions of the residence permit are observed. The Court found that because registration had replaced the institution of the residence permit, its absence could not serve as grounds for restricting, or its existence as a basis for realizing, civil rights and freedoms, including the right to housing.

The reason for hearing the other case was not only citizens' complaints but also an inquiry of the court of general jurisdiction, which concluded that there was a disparity between the requirements of the Housing Code and the Constitution. Under the Housing Code, accommodations are kept for a tenant who is temporarily absent and for members of his family for a period of only six months. Then, according to Article 61 of the code, the tenant may be found to have lost the right to these accommodations. In a ruling of June 23, 1995, the Court found unconstitutional those provisions of the code that limit the right to accommodation because of the citizen's temporary absence due to imprisonment, and serve as grounds for depriving the citizen of the right to accommodation. The claimants had been deprived of this right because they had been sentenced to imprisonment.

There was a dissent in this case. Justice Yu. M. Danilov concluded that the challenged provisions of the Housing Code did not contradict the Constitution. Justice Danilov stated in his dissenting opinion that "losing the right to certain accommodations does not entail losing the civil right to housing: a citizen may realize this right at any time, either by concluding a new contract or through legal proceedings. The Housing Code contains the necessary legal mechanisms to prohibit arbitrary deprivation of housing. The grounds on which a citizen may be found to have lost his right to accommodations are clearly stated, and a judicial remedy is envisaged (Article 61)."

The procedure for inheriting the property of collective-farm households was considered by the Court in a case involving Article 560, Sections 1 and 2 of the Russian Federation's Civil Code in connection with A. B. Naumov's claim (ruling of January 16, 1996). The claimant was denied relief by the court of general jurisdiction (in a case involving property rights to part of a house) on the basis of Article 560, Section 1 of the Civil Code, which provides that in the case of the death of a member of a collective-farm household, there is no inheritance of the household's property. The Court, recognizing that the institution of the collective-farm household had lost its legal basis both in land legislation and in new civil legislation, and also recognizing that a special procedure for inheritance in a collective-farm household had made the right of inheritance guaranteed by the Constitution impossible as a practical matter, found the challenged rule and related rules unconstitutional.

Justice N. V. Vitruk, in dissent, contended that the rules of the Civil Code conformed to the Constitution because they "do not disclaim and impair the right of inheritance in a collective-farm household, and restrictions connected with a special procedure of implementation are stated by law in order to protect the rights and lawful interests of other collective-farm household members." The justice also argued that the Court, by not recognizing a collective-farm household as a subject of law, went beyond the framework of its powers, as it "virtually took upon itself the function of the legislature."

Constitutional Protection of the Right of Citizenship

On May 16, 1996, the Constitutional Court ruled in favor of an individual whose claim of citizenship had been reviewed by every lower court. The case involved Article 18, item "g" of the law "On

Citizenship of the Russian Federation" in connection with V. A. Smirnov's complaint. Smirnov was born and lived in the Russian Federation, then lived in Lithuania for a number of years, and returned to Russia as a permanent resident after February 6, 1992.[7] He was denied a supplementary sheet in his Soviet passport certifying his Russian citizenship. All the courts, including the Supreme Court, denied his claim. The Constitutional Court, having studied the record, noted that the lower courts, on the basis of Article 13, Section 1 and Article 18, item "g" of the law of citizenship, considered Smirnov to have lost Russian citizenship because he had the right to acquire citizenship only through the procedure of registration. The Court disagreed. It stated that the presence of a citizen of the former USSR outside the Russian Federation at the moment when the law on citizenship came into force could be considered a condition for Russian citizenship through registration only if that person was not a citizen of the Russian Federation by birth. According to Article 13, Smirnov was within the category of persons who were born on or after December 30, 1922,[8] and later lost their status as citizens of the former USSR. Such persons are considered to be citizens of Russia by birth if they were born within the borders of the Russian Federation. Thus, Smirnov was a citizen of Russia by birth. Not only was he such by birth, before he lost his Soviet citizenship, but he remained such, until the time when he should wish to change his citizenship. In justifying its ruling, the Court stressed that persons in this category, such as Smirnov, did not lose Russian citizenship "solely by virtue of the fact of residence outside the Russian Federation at the moment of the law's coming into force, because Article 4 states that residence of a citizen of the Russian Federation outside the country does not terminate Russian citizenship." Therefore, the Court found the challenged provision of the law on citizenship unconstitutional. At the same time it agreed

7. The federal law "On Citizenship of the Russian Federation" became effective on this day.

8. The establishment of the Soviet Union was proclaimed on this day.

with the necessity of registration for citizens of the Russian Federation who have lived outside Russia, to give notice that they have returned to Russian territory for permanent residence, that they have not expressed a wish to terminate their Russian citizenship by birth, and that they do not hold citizenship in another state that was part of the former USSR. This "notifying registration" is solely for record-keeping purposes and not a condition on which "the availability or unavailability of citizenship in the Russian Federation depends."

Constitutional Protection of Freedom of Movement,
the Right to Leave the Country, and the Right
of Stateless Persons to Freedom and Personal Inviolability

Two recent cases of the Constitutional Court illustrate how some administrative bodies entrusted with certain functions have explicitly or implicitly violated human rights and liberties guaranteed by the Constitution.

The Court found a number of statutes enacted in Moscow and the Moscow and Stavropol' regions making the exercise of the constitutional right to freedom of movement and choice of a place of residence contingent upon the payment of certain dues unconstitutional insofar as they violated the constitutional principles of equality and restricted fundamental human and civil rights and freedoms (ruling of April 4, 1996).

On January 15, 1998, the Constitutional Court examined a case involving Article 8, Sections 1 and 3 of the federal law "On the Procedure of Departure from and Entry into the Russian Federation." Russian citizen A. Ya. Avanov claimed a violation of his constitutional right to leave Russia freely. The complainant, who had a permanent residence permit based on his residence in Tbilisi (in the Republic of Georgia, formerly part of the USSR), in fact had been living in Moscow for many years. In 1996, he applied to the Department of Visas and Permits of Moscow's Main Department of the Interior for an external passport. The passport was denied because he lacked a place of abode, the availability of which would allow him to be registered in Moscow. The Tver Intermunicipal Court (the lower court of general jurisdiction), where the complainant applied, also denied his claim on the basis of Article 8 of the federal law mentioned above. The court observed that the complainant had a right to apply for a passport only to an agency of the Republic of Georgia, on the basis of his residence outside the Russian Federation.

The Constitutional Court held that constitutional rights and freedoms are guaranteed to citizens regardless of their place of residence or the availability or unavailability of accommodations for permanent or temporary residence, because the state is not obliged to provide citizens with accommodations. The Court emphasized that exercise of the civil right to leave the country freely and, thus, to obtain a passport for foreign travel, must not depend on the availability or unavailability of accommodations. The Court drew attention to the fact that the issuance of a passport only in accordance with the place of residence is discriminatory and thus contradicts Article 19, Sections 1 and 2 of the Constitution, which guarantees equality of human and civil rights and freedoms regardless of the citizen's place of residence, and regardless of the availability or unavailability of registration according to place of residence. According to Article 3 of the federal law "On the Right of Citizens of the Russian Federation to Free Movement and Choice of Place of Residence or Domicile within the Borders of the Russian Federation," registration or its unavailability cannot serve as grounds for restriction or as a condition for exercise of civil rights and freedoms envisaged by the Constitution and the laws of the Russian Federation, as well as the constitutions and laws of the republics that are constituent parts of the Russian Federation.

The Russian Constitution admits the possibility of restricting civil and human rights and freedoms by federal law only to the extent necessary to protect the fundamentals of the constitutional system; the morals, health, rights, and lawful interests of other individuals; the country's defense capability; and the security of the state. Certain restrictions are stated in the federal law "On the Procedure of Departure from and Entry into the Russian Federation."

This law contains an exhaustive list of cases in which the right of a citizen of the Russian Federation to leave the country may be restricted temporarily. In particular, restrictions are established for persons with access to information considered a state secret, persons drafted into military service, suspects, convicts, persons avoiding performance of obligations imposed by the court, and persons who presented false information when drawing up documents. However, all these restrictions operate without regard to the citizen's place of residence or stay and the availability or unavailability of registration.

In its judgment on the second case involving Article 31, Section 2 of the Soviet law of June 24, 1981, "On the Legal Status of Foreign Citizens in the USSR," in connection with Iakh'ia Dashti Gafur's complaint, the Constitutional Court found unconstitutional a challenged provision under which a foreign citizen or a stateless person who is to be expelled from the Russian Federation, and who attempts to avoid departure, is subject to the prosecutor's sanction of detention for the period of time necessary for expulsion, when such detention exceeds forty-eight hours and no judgment is rendered (ruling of February 17, 1998).

The facts of this case were the following: Iakh'ia Dashti Gafur, a stateless person residing in the Russian Federation, was apprehended and detained on February 18, 1997, on the basis of a ruling by the Department of Visas and Permits of Moscow's Main Department of the Interior, sanctioned by the Prosecutor of Moscow, requiring his escorted expulsion from the Russian Federation. For more than two months he was held in custody by the Social Rehabilitation Center of Moscow's Main Department of the Interior, and on April 29, 1997, he was forcibly deported to Sweden. The ruling on his expulsion was based on Article 31, Section 2 of the Soviet law "On the Legal Status of Foreign Citizens in the USSR," which requires a foreign citizen or stateless person to leave the country during the period of time specified in the decision on expulsion. A person who avoids departure is subject, with the prosecutor's sanction, to detention and forcible expulsion, detention being allowed for the period of time necessary for expulsion.

The Court found, however, that the Constitution establishes the right of every person (including foreign citizens and stateless persons) to freedom and personal inviolability and permits apprehension and detention only in accordance with a judgment. Until the judgment has been handed down, a person cannot be detained for more than forty-eight hours. As a result, a foreign citizen or a stateless person within the borders of the Russian Federation, if he is to be forcibly expelled from the country, can be detained prior to a judgment solely for the period of time necessary for expulsion but not more than forty-eight hours. A person may be held in excess of forty-eight hours only in accordance with a judgment and only if expulsion cannot be carried out without such detention. The ruling stresses that "a judgment must guarantee protection for a person not only against arbitrary prolongation of the detention period in excess of forty-eight hours, but also against unlawful detention itself, because a court in any case assesses the lawfulness of, and grounds for, detention of every person." Detention for an indefinite period of time cannot be considered an admissible restriction of the right to freedom and personal inviolability; rather, it is an impairment of that right. The challenged provision of the Soviet law on detention for the period necessary for expulsion may thus not be considered grounds for detention for an indefinite period, even when deciding the issue of a stateless person and when expulsion is delayed because no state agrees to admit the person being expelled. "Otherwise, detention as a necessary measure of executing a decision on expulsion could turn into an independent form of punishment not envisaged by the Russian Federation's legislation and contradicting . . . the rules of the Constitution of the Russian Federation."

Conclusion

Analysis of the cases discussed indicates that the Constitutional Court protects rights and freedoms regardless of any circumstances that may serve – and, unfortunately, have served, when unlawful decisions were made by state bodies prior to judicial involvement – to justify infringement of the citizen's interest, in the widest sense. For example, in the two decisions above, the Court declined to take into account the lack of a permanent place of residence and the lack of Russian citizenship in protecting the claimants' rights. Here it is important to emphasize that, in accordance with the law "On the Constitutional Court," if the Court, on examining the constitutionality of a law, finds that the law, as applied, is unconstitutional, the case is subject to review by a competent body. Moreover, the legal expenses of citizens and their associations are subject to reimbursement in accordance with established procedures. Meaningful guarantees of the exercise of human and civil rights and freedoms guaranteed in the Constitution are thus being established.

The Russian Constitution, as mentioned above, envisages the possibility that personal rights and freedoms may be restricted. The Constitution defines the areas in which rights and freedoms may be restricted and the form of the legal action creating such restrictions; that is, the federal law. Federal law passes through a number of stages before coming into force: adoption of the law by the State Duma, approval by the Federation Council, and, finally, signature and promulgation by the president. These measures are to some degree additional guarantees against arbitrary and unjustified restriction of rights and freedoms.

In addition, Article 56 of the Constitution contemplates the possibility of restricting rights and freedoms in a state of emergency. Under this article, certain restrictions of rights and freedoms may be established in a state of emergency. The limits and terms of these restrictions are articulated. These restrictions are aimed at ensuring the security of citizens and protecting the constitutional system, and they are in accordance with federal constitutional law.

As may be seen, guarantees of personal rights and freedoms are enhanced by the introduction of another form of legal action restricting rights and freedoms: federal constitutional law. Article 56, Section 3 of the Constitution in particular makes clear that under no condition are the following rights and freedoms subject to restriction: the right to life, the right to personal dignity, the right of privacy, freedom of conscience, the right of entrepreneurship and other business activity not prohibited by law, the right to housing, and the right of legal relief.

Establishing certain limits in constitutional legislation for the restriction of personal rights and freedoms is essential to ensure their free development and exercise without threat of suppression by the state. At the same time, human rights and freedoms are violated in Russia, as is evident both in legislation and executive regulations and in their application by state and local bodies. In this regard, the activity of the Constitutional Court is extremely important. The prerogative of the Court and strict compliance with its rulings undoubtedly will help to bring Russian society closer to a democratic state where the rule of law prevails and where man and his rights and liberties have the highest value.

SOME HISTORICAL AND POLITICAL ASPECTS OF BUILDING A CIVIL SOCIETY IN RUSSIA

SERGEI KOMARITSYN

Sergei Komaritsyn is the editor of the Evening Krasnoiarsk, *an independent newspaper serving the central Siberian region. He is deeply involved in defending freedom of the press and in fostering the development of civil society. In his remarks here, Mr. Komaritsyn uses the Krasnoiarsk region as a model for current developments affecting the mass media, civil society, and the evolution of the political situation in Russia.*

RUSSIA IS A COUNTRY with a very young ethos and a very young state. Russia's neighbors in both the East and the West either have recorded several thousand years of independent history, as in the case of China, or have developed from the civilizations of classical antiquity, as in the case of many European nations. Unlike a number of Slavic and Baltic countries with a similar history that have succeeded – albeit not without problems – in becoming integrated into Europe, the Old Russian state's process of integration was interrupted by the Mongol invasion. The legacy of the Mongol period has not been overcome to the present day. Muscovite Russia did not become a savage Asiatic power, but it did not become a country with European customs, either.

The principal historic task facing Russia over the past three hundred years was modernization. The chief instrument of this modernization was always the state. Whereas industrial development in the countries of western and central Europe took place unaided, "from below," in Russia it was achieved with the help of state institutions, "from above." Tsarist Russia did not succeed in solving the problem of industrial transition, however. This task was accomplished by Soviet Russia, at the price of huge sacrifices and historical costs. The industrial transition in Russia was accomplished under the Bolsheviks, whose main instrument again was the state. Russia was transformed into a predominantly urbanized country with a sufficiently high level of education and with serious industrial and scientific potential. At that time, however, a series of technological revolutions in Europe and the United States brought the West to a fundamentally new level of economic development. Russia was faced with a new task: postindustrial transition. All attempts to attain this goal by using the same basic tool – the state – proved ineffective, however. This situation first resulted in the reforms undertaken by Gorbachev, then produced a profound systemic crisis, followed by the disintegration of the Soviet Union.

Over the course of Russian history, especially the history of the twentieth century, the supremacy of the state is incontestable. The role of the state has hypertrophied, however, to the detriment of the development of civil society. A civil society is above all an urban society. And it was in the cities of medieval Europe that present-day democracy originated. It was there that the elements of self-government arose, along with the principle of separation of powers, universities as self-governing communities, the first public organizations, and, later, a free press. A Russian city was primarily an administrative and military center, by no means a center of handicraft and trade. And though in some European countries the urban and rural populations were equal in number as early as the fifteenth and sixteenth centuries, in Russia this was not true until the 1960s, only half a century after the elimination of widespread illiteracy among the overwhelming majority of the population. Over the life of one generation, three-fourths of the country's population was resettled from the country to the city. For this and other reasons, urban traditions, urban culture, and contemporary political culture in Russia differ from established practices in Europe and North America.

In addition, the collective, or cooperative production unit, was a basic component of society in Russia for many decades. It was in the collective that people not only solved the majority of their personal and family problems, but also engaged in grass-roots social activism. In the absence of a parliamentary system, a multiparty political system, and freedom of the press, the collective, for a majority of the population, played the role of the institutions of a quasi-civil society. At the same time, in the social structure, the relative density of the self-employed workers, members of "free" professions, and scientific and creative workers increased. And in these groups the relationships of a civil society existed. For this reason, the scientific and creative intelligentsia became the social basis and driving force of Gorbachev's *perestroika,* which the intelligentsia understood as the path toward a state ruled by law and a civil society. These social groups turned out to be politically weak, however, and they were unable to exert control over the process of reform. It became uncontrolled, then chaotic. The rapid political reform of the Gorbachev era was not accompanied by adequate changes in the economy; as a result, stability was lost and the Soviet Union ceased to exist.

The aim of Gorbachev's successors was to separate the economy from the state. The Russian monetarists thought that a self-regulating market would stabilize the economy and lead to economic growth, but in Russian conditions this idea did not work because of the absence of a market. The hasty and total privatization of property and the redirecting of financial reserves into private structures during the formation of the banking system did not lead to the functioning of market mechanisms; on the contrary, these actions impeded their growth, created oligarchic groups, and contributed to the criminalization of a substantial part of the economy. That, in turn, interfered with the formation of the institutions of civil society in Russia. Moreover, the monetarist government made commitments to international financial organizations – the World Bank, the IMF, and the IBRD – whose experts stipulated, as a condition of the foreign loans, that inflation be suppressed by reduction of the money supply. According to figures from the Russian Central Bank, the relative volume of the money supply was reduced by a factor of eight over a six-year period. This circumstance suppressed Russia's industrial development; resulted in debt and nonpayment, surrogate money circulation, and impracticably high interest rates on state securities; and, finally, led in August 1998 to a severe financial crisis and the threat of default. Moreover, the relations created as a result of this government policy are not in fact market relations.

Nevertheless, in the 1990s market relations continued to develop, and millions of people found themselves engaged in the small and medium-sized business sector. It was from these people that the Russian "middle class" was formed. Even the oligarchs played a certain positive role in this development, by hiring highly paid managers, experts, and consultants, who in their turn provided work for private schools, law firms, tourist agencies, advertising agencies, and the entertainment sector. And it is the "middle class" that is the social base and main vehicle of the ideas of civil society. The Russian "middle class" suffered severely in August 1998, however.

The vector of Russia's historic growth has already been determined; the country is moving in the direction of creating an effective market economy and a democratic society. Not one of the political forces with real influence has any doubt of that. All of them understand the necessity of modernization. That excludes the possibility of a return of the communist regime. These processes have become irreversible. In the short term, however, there may be different ways of implementing this modernization, including the possibility of a prolonged oligarchic period or a phase with elements of authoritarian rule, during which restrictions of democratic freedoms are possible.

The main question in Russia today has to do with power. The current situation suits neither the population of the country nor the political forces. Therefore, the essence of political life in Russia now is the electoral campaign that no one has yet announced. In Russia's present-day political system, a key role is played by the president, whose power – though limited by objective circumstances – still is decisive in many regards. It is the president who forms the government and selects political strategy. Therefore the struggle is primarily over that office. There are several realistic candidates for the presidency in Russia now, and all the influential groups in Russian society are faced with choosing which of them they will support. Each of them has his own public and political backing. They include Iurii Luzhkov, Gennadii Ziuganov, Aleksandr Lebed', and Evgenii Primakov. The remaining candidates have no realistic chance of becoming president, but they can influence the concrete results of the elections. Although, according to many sociological polls, the highest rating among those four goes to Gennadii Ziuganov, he actually has the least chance of winning. This is due first to the limited size of the Communist electorate (no more than 25 percent of all voters), a portion of which represents a protest vote that could switch to Aleksandr Lebed'. Moreover, the Communist Party itself is undergoing a crisis. It is increasingly hard for Ziuganov to balance between the extreme positions in his party itself. He also failed to overcome the conflict between the Communist Party of the Russian Federation (CPRF) as a whole and the CPRF faction in the State Duma. Despite the radical phraseology (an ideological tribute to the voters), the Communist faction in the Duma has become fully integrated into the political party system. It is completely satisfied with the role of the parliamentary opposition. In essence, in terms of their political views and the decisions made in the Duma, a majority of the Communist deputies are right-wing social democrats of the European type. Moreover, there are some "Communist oligarchs" among them – people who hold substantial personal property and have no interest in nationalization or any other anti-market measures. At the same time, the rank-and-file members of the Communist Party are basically people of an older generation who were placed in unfavorable circumstances, and many of them are below the "poverty line." They demand radical reforms, which they understand as the redistribution of means for the benefit of the poor. The pressure of the party's broad masses makes the policy of the CPRF extremely inconsistent. These internal contradictions do not suit the CPRF leadership; a split has become apparent. In the upcoming elections to the Duma, the fundamentalist wing of the party (Il'iukhin, Makashov, and others) plans to participate independently. At the same time, the party intellectuals who lean toward European right-wing socialism (Podberezkin, Seleznev, and others) also want to participate independently of the CPRF, and their statements indicate that they generally are going to support Iurii Luzhkov.

Luzhkov is the most acceptable candidate for the intelligentsia, the regional elites, and the "middle class." He has sufficiently broad public support, and part of the left-leaning Communist electorate, part of Grigorii Iavlinskii's electorate, and even part of the voters leaning toward the right-wing liberal parties are prepared to vote for him, since the remaining realistic candidates are simply unacceptable to them. Iurii Luzhkov is the only leader in Russia who has consistently tried to build a "middle class" while at the same time implementing social programs. Small businesses make up 55 percent of Moscow's budget. This is not true in any other region: in the Krasnoiarsk region *(krai),* for example, half the budget is made up by two enterprises, the Noril'sk mining and metallurgical complex and an aluminum plant. In Moscow, 100 percent of the taxes owed are collected; this is the highest rate of collection in the country. The situation has resulted in the creation of a milieu, a "middle class," in the capital.

Luzhkov, despite his "left-wing" phraseology, is a typical supporter of the market and a proponent of the growth of democracy. He does not have enough leverage in terms of information flow, however, and his opponents have succeeded to a substantial degree in molding public opinion in the provinces, in creating a belief that Moscow lives "high on the hog" at the expense of the other regions and the country as a whole. That notion will be an indisputable minus in his election campaign. Moreover, Luzhkov is in conflict with very powerful oligarchs – people in finance and in oil and gas – who control enormous resources and will do everything in their power to oppose the Moscow mayor because they are worried about their future.

One additional minus for Luzhkov is Premier Primakov. After the fall of Chernomyrdin and the failure of "the party of power," represented by the organization *Nash Dom – Rossiia* [Our House Is Russia], a majority of the administrative elite – from the Novosibirsk Communist governor Mukha to the Iaroslavl liberal governor Lisitsyn – swore allegiance to *Otechestvo* [Fatherland], Luzhkov's party. However, the hypothetical possibility of Evgenii Primakov's putting himself forward as a candidate for the presidency disturbs the process of consolidating the administrative elite in support of Luzhkov. For this elite, Primakov is a figure equal in value to Luzhkov, perhaps even preferable. Moreover, Primakov now is the most popular politician in Russia; he has authority in practically all levels of society. Primakov, Luzhkov, and Ziuganov all are predictable politicians; their views and programs are well understood, and it is clear whom they will look to for support and what policy they will pursue.

The situation of General Lebed' is much more complicated. Little is known about the people in his circle, and the sources and linchpins of his influence on the political process are hidden from the public eye. He has no economic views; it is impossible to trace his attachment to any particular philosophy or view of life. He cannot lead the civil authorities. At the same time, Lebed' has sufficiently great support from people who are tired of the incompleteness of the reforms in Russia, who want clear, simple solutions, who want "order." For a long time, an artificial image was cultivated for Lebed': the "Russian Pinochet – terrible outside, good inside," a person capable of fighting the criminal element, capable of maintaining order "with an iron hand."

In the elections, the following groups of the population will support Lebed': people with a low level of education, who are very susceptible to political myths; the protest vote; practically all of Zhirinovskii's former constituency; and part of the Communist electorate. Lebed' also has the hidden support of very influential forces in Russia, though this support has diminished somewhat lately. Nevertheless, the strength of his backers was demonstrated quite clearly in the election of the governor of the Krasnoiarsk region. There is a belief, not unfounded, that the people closest to President Yeltsin in

1998 gambled on Lebed' as the future president of Russia, who could guarantee them the protection of their present status and their business. In 1998, the election of a person from the "party of power" as president was considered impossible, so these members of Yeltsin's circle began to create a politician from outside the system with the image of a defender of the nation, a member of the opposition. General Lebed' fits this role better than anyone else. It is possible that some kind of agreement, perhaps an oral one, was worked out among them. Otherwise, it is impossible to understand why the president's administration, many government structures, and the most powerful television channel (50 percent of whose shares are owned by the state) supported Lebed' in the Krasnoiarsk election.

If Lebed' is a member of the opposition, then why did he easily succeed, after the victory in the election, in replacing powerful officials in Krasnoiarsk who were directly subordinate to Moscow and putting his own underlings in their places? A former assistant of Lebed's was even appointed as the president's representative for the Krasnoiarsk region, an appointment only the president of the country can make by decree. And this was by no means the only case in recent Russian history when someone other than a local resident was appointed as the president's representative. The representative has very broad authority; he has responsibility for federal property within the region and coordinates the work of the special services.

Recently, after Valentin Iumashev left the president's administration, this structure's support of Lebed' lessened somewhat. But the struggle of Primakov's government against Boris Berezovskii left Lebed' facing a choice: whose side to take. It would seem that Berezovskii also will cease to be a Lebed' ally.

Lebed' is not simply a political myth. We now can assess him on the basis of actual experience. First, there is the electoral campaign in Krasnoiarsk. It was the most expensive and the dirtiest electoral campaign in Russia. Huge amounts of money were received from unknown sources, and the funds were used to pay for tens of thousands of volunteers and an enormous amount of campaign literature. Even Lebed' said this was "gray" money, funds derived from tax evasion. The most underhanded methods were used, including methods of psychological warfare: insinuations, lies, forgery, slander, and provocation. Falsified literature was published on behalf of the campaign staff of Lebed's rival, and there were spurious letters accusing Lebed's opponent of theft and homosexuality.

Lebed' won in the Krasnoiarsk region as a whole, but he lost in the city of Krasnoiarsk, where public attitudes are more stable and democratic values are more pronounced among the population.

Over the course of his government Lebed' has destroyed the region's ability to function. All the economic indicators have deteriorated sharply. He has made up his administration of casual workers who have neither professional experience nor knowledge of the region. Four or five times in six months, Lebed' has replaced deputies responsible for key areas: economics, finance, the social sector. After half a year we already have our fifth regional minister of finance and our fifth minister of economics. He has quarreled with the region's entire legislative body, where there once existed a faction of the movement bearing his name. He has created conflicts with the local business elite. Even the local party, which bore the honorific "Honor and the Motherland – Aleksandr Lebed'," has disavowed him. He has not fulfilled a single one of his campaign promises. Finally, he has made an attempt to set up a police regime in the region.

Many people in Krasnoiarsk think that the arrests and accusations of corruption involving former regional officials are wrongful and political in nature. An atmosphere of fear and suspicion has been created in the region. The people surrounding Lebed' have used blackmail, threats, and intimidation in their dealings with the press. Pressure was put on all the newspapers and television stations that were critical of the policies of Lebed's administration. That includes the *Evening Krasnoiarsk,* of which I am the editor. They tried to buy up the paper's debts, threatened the reporters, and tried to institute criminal proceedings against me for publishing investigative journalism. Lebed' has succeeded in firing the director of the local state television station. Nevertheless, today Krasnoiarsk's free, nongovernment press in its entirety is in opposition to General Lebed'.

At the same time, the Krasnoiarsk region finds itself subject to an information blockade. The publications of the Krasnoiarsk press are radically different from what the general Russian newspapers – with the exception of *Izvestia* – write and what the general Russian television stations show. Outside the borders of Krasnoiarsk, people in Russia don't know what is actually happening in the region. In the rest of Russia, as before, the myth of Lebed' is alive. One of the reasons for such a state of affairs is the fact that, in contradistinction to the regional press, the general Russian press is run by oligarchs, many of whom supported, and continue to support, Lebed'. Moreover, Lebed' and his image makers have succeeded in transforming information to make it appear that social conflict in the region is nothing more than resistance to Lebed' on the part of local businessmen, whom they present as gangsters. That only reinforces the myth of Lebed' as someone who fights the mafia, someone capable of "putting things in order." His ratings as a presidential candidate are on the upswing.

The creation of the Lebed' myth has also been assisted by foreign politicians and statesmen who like to meet with the governor of Krasnoiarsk. As a result, even literate people in other areas of Russia sincerely believe that Aleksandr Lebed' is attracting huge amounts of foreign investment to the Krasnoiarsk region. Actually, Lebed' always talks about foreign investment, but so far not a single cent has come into the region as a result of his activities.

The enormous gap between the image of General Lebed' in the other areas of Russia and his reputation in the Krasnoiarsk region bears witness to the fact that the public consciousness in Russia is subject to great manipulation. It is precisely that kind of manipulation that represents the chief danger for civil society in Russia and for the strengthening of democratic customs.

As the presidential elections approach, the situation evidently will become exacerbated. Possible changes in the distribution of political forces, weakening of the oligarchs, and the results of the activities of Primakov's government – whether positive or negative – can alter the overall situation. No new aspirants to the office of president will appear. Unfortunately, the state of civil society in Russia is such that any acceleration or slowing of the process of developing the institutions of civil society and spreading democratic values depends largely on the political figure who will occupy the chief office in the Kremlin. The presidential election and, to some extent, the parliamentary elections will mark a boundary. Beyond that point history will record either an improvement or a worsening of the country's economic situation, as well as changes affecting law and order, civil rights, and the strengthening of democratic principles. In this respect, the elections of 2000 will be significantly more important than the 1996 elections.

RUSSIA'S LEGAL REVOLUTION

SARAH CAREY

Sarah Carey is a senior partner at the Washington, D.C., law firm of Squire, Sanders & Dempsey. For the past decade her practice has focused on negotiation and on the structuring of trade and investment transactions in Russia and the Newly Independent States. She also chairs the board of the Eurasia Foundation, a grant-making body created by the United States Congress to support economic and democratic reform in this geographic region. In this chapter, Ms. Carey addresses developments in commercial and contract law in Russia since the fall of Soviet Communism.

HE FIRST PHASE of the legal revolution in Russia made possible the creation and operation of a free market economy. Today the country has the full range of laws required for the operation of viable private enterprises. Although most of these laws are not exactly what Americans would consider ideal, they meet international standards. The second phase, now under way, involves not so much the passage of new laws as the development of understanding and respect for existing ones. The "genetic coding" that Boris Pustintsev mentioned[1] is far from complete, and there is a need to strengthen and make more effective the enforcement of existing laws.

I currently chair a group of twenty lawyers who work on various kinds of investments and commercial transactions in Russia. The group consists of attorneys based in a Moscow office as well as an American contingent, and the firm has been in Moscow for approximately ten years. Here are four examples of the kind of work these attorneys are doing: First, we are working with a large Dutch packaging company that is building steel drums for the petroleum

1. See "Bring Out Your Dead!" by Boris Pustintsev, pp. 3–16 in this volume.

industry and producing other packaging for consumer goods for Lever Brothers. The company plans to create or purchase two dozen manufacturing enterprises in Russia before 2005. Second, we are advising a large minerals trading company in regard to the creation of a vertically integrated copper company. Third, we are litigating on behalf of American shareholders whose RosTelecom stock, valued at about $12 million, was stolen through fraud committed on the registrar several years ago. Fourth, we serve as advisors to Russia's leading fashion designer with regard to the structuring of his companies and the protection of his intellectual property rights in Russia, France, Italy, and the United States. I mention these activities not to promote the firm in which I am a partner, but to illustrate the complexity of the legal activity being done in our small Russian office alone. Dozens of other major American law firms are engaged in similar work, none of which would have been possible ten, or even seven years ago.

In my capacity as chair of the board of the Eurasia Foundation, I recently met with the talented bilateral, bicultural staff members of the foundation's Moscow office, who are working on projects designed to stimulate new forms of economic development in the region. This American-led operation, deeply involved in helping the region's economy to progress, is being welcomed with open arms.

Often, centering our attention on the more sensational rumors and realities of life in Russia today – a focus encouraged by press reports – Americans overlook the extraordinary things that have been accomplished. Many of the contributors to this book have commented on the changes within the commercial code, and some have pointed out that Russia's legal tradition did not really develop until the reign of Tsar Alexander II. There was comparatively little philosophical or other legal scholarship, just a few codes and the like, with none of the intellectual underpinnings found in the West. There were no fundamental doctrines that defined the relationship between man and the state or between man and property, for example. Consequently, one does not find the depth of experience that the Anglo-American tradition offers. In addition, many of the gains made in the nineteenth century were undermined, if not totally eradicated, by the Bolsheviks, who believed that the state and the law were unnecessary. Therefore, the Bolsheviks concluded, these creations ought to disappear when social classes were eliminated.

Strangely, a period of legal reform occurred under Stalin and again under Khrushchev. Successful efforts were made, in the Stalin era, for example, to enact certain codes and introduce certain fundamentals of legal procedure. From the perspective of a market economy these laws seem satisfactory; the underlying concepts are sound, by and large. Scrutiny of the system as a whole, however, reveals two major flaws.

First, the Communist Party reigned supreme and exerted control over the entire legal system, particularly the courts. Second, the state ran the economy. The state, acting as Mr. Business, controlled the assets, ran the companies, and even directed the day-to-day operations of factories. Private enterprise was largely illegal. Therefore, although the laws appeared to be adequate, they did not apply to the private sector because no such sector was allowed to exist. Private activity was meager and confined within strict limits.

Private enterprise really started under Mikhail Gorbachev, even before the 1988 Party Congress at which he declared his intention to create a society based on law. Using the existing legal system, he initiated certain new principles and new decrees that opened the starting gate, so to speak, for private individuals who wanted to become involved in economic activity.

In 1987, Gorbachev introduced two important new laws: the joint venture decree and the decree on cooperatives. The former, a four-page law, allowed foreign investors to join with a Russian partner in setting up a Russian company owned not by the state but by the people who set up the company. The investors were to govern their own company in terms of decision making, and they alone were responsible for its obligations and expenditures. The state would not stand behind them; instead, this statute was based on the concept of *khozraschet,* financial autonomy and independence. Businesses were to operate on a self-sustaining basis. This notion was radical, and people who looked at the statute – including companies represented by my firm – thought, Fine, here's an island of private commercial activity, but these companies still are surrounded by a sea of "*Gos*"[2] organizations. Private companies had to operate in an economy that was dictated and controlled by the government. How were they able to accomplish that? They succeeded because the concepts reflected in the joint venture law, in the law on enterprises that was passed at about the same time, and in the law on cooperatives, represented principles that were being embraced with accelerating speed. Their swift acceptance was the basis for the emergence of all the private business forms required by a free market economy.

There ensued a tremendous amount of commercial activity in Moscow: cooperative restaurants, travel agencies, and beauty parlors began to spring up. Certainly, as far as foreigners were concerned, there was enormous interest in joint ventures, and many such ventures were launched. As the new concepts of *khozraschet* and the ability to control the decision making of one's own company were evolving, certain state apparatuses were being abolished. The Ministry of Foreign Trade, which had held a monopoly on foreign trade, was eliminated overnight. Immediately, all sorts of enterprises and government entities could trade on their own directly with foreigners. The absence of state control resulted in a frenzy of wheeling and dealing and in the creation of unsustainable financial liabilities. By becoming middlemen in this new trading system, many Russians became millionaires overnight. Shortly after the Ministry of Foreign Trade was eliminated, many other ministries and state organizations began to disappear.

The scholars among our speakers here can endow this busy and confused period with order, perhaps. Along with my firm's clients, however, I found myself in the midst of a hurricane of change and

2. "*Gos*" is the abbreviated form of the adjective *gosudarstvennyi,* meaning "state (-controlled)" or "public," as in Gosplan (State Planning Commission) or Goskomtrud (State Labor Commission).

activity. We would go to Gosplan to get something approved, and the candid gentlemen scheduled to meet with us would announce that they would not be employed there the following day. On one occasion we represented Delta Airlines in the takeover of Pan Am's Moscow routes. Everything regarding a foreign airline – routes, landing rights, the rights of crew members, everything else that was needed – had been the responsibility of the Ministry of Civil Aviation. When we went to meet with the deputy who had been responsible for Pan Am, he threw up his hands. Not only was the ministry's task being redefined, he told us, but the ministry would no longer own the airports, which were becoming independent. Moreover – God forbid! – new independent regional airlines were emerging.

For the people in the middle of this revolution, it was truly an extraordinary time. Remarkably, many were able to cope with the volume and pace of change, all of which was based on short, sometimes flimsy decrees, rules, and laws: not the two-thousand-page tomes that the U.S. Congress enacts, but short concept papers, in effect. It is difficult to overestimate the impact of the new laws that permitted and nurtured the creation of private businesses in the late 1980s. When the Soviet Union collapsed and Russia emerged in late December 1991, scholars continued to work on drafting new laws to support market reform and the private sector. Initially it was difficult to obtain copies of these laws, but now everything, including court decisions, is readily available on CD-ROM. From 1991 through 1995 or 1996, Russia was governed largely through emergency decree. This period saw enactment of many of the basic laws required to place the economy in private hands and to protect investors. For example, the first basic privatization law, best described as a blockbuster, was enacted in 1991. In a moment I will touch more on the laws regarding privatization, but now I wish to address other aspects of the legal revolution.

In 1992, Russia saw enactment of laws on foreign investment, laws regulating currency transactions and the banking sector, and laws on consumer protection. The following year, three or four laws modernized the protection of intellectual property. By passing these laws and by subsequently acceding to various international treaties, Russia set up a regime that, on paper at least, meets international standards for the protection of intellectual property. In the same year, 1993, the new Constitution was passed. Later I will elaborate on some of the unique, confidence-building provisions that are included in the Constitution and their impact on private-sector activity.

Soon thereafter, an entire regime for regulation of securities was enacted, along with continuous improvements of laws previously passed. In 1990, for example, there had been a decree on joint stock companies. In 1995, the Duma improved on it by enacting a major law on joint stock companies, which now is the basic corporate law. A civil code, parts one and two of which are currently in effect, was enacted in 1994 and 1995. These three laws – the two parts of the civil code and the joint stock company law – provide all the corporate law necessary. They are the first tomes to be consulted by any investor, by anyone setting up a company, buying assets, acquiring stock, or purchasing securities.

There has been much criticism of the role of foreign assistance to Russia in the privatization process and in some other aspects of reform, but immense assistance in the drafting of the country's civil codes was provided, and with great wisdom, by Europe and the United States. It was a monumental achievement to bring those laws into existence. They provide extensive protections for investors; in fact, shareholder protections under the joint stock company law in Russia are probably stronger on paper than the protections offered in the United States. The provisions ensuring shareholder democracy, too, are strong.

At the same time that enabling legislation was being enacted to allow private citizens to set up businesses or buy existing ones, other regulatory laws were being enacted to protect the public from evildoing in the economy. Into this category fall the consumer protection law, the anti-monopoly law, improvements in the environmental laws, and the securities laws protecting investors. All this was achieved in a very brief time, and sometimes it was not fully "digested," or – to use Boris Pustintsev's term again – "genetically coded." Moreover, laws on dispute resolution and laws defining the arbitrage courts and other courts were being enacted at the same time. It is hard for us to comprehend this legal revolution, because in our system today major changes in law come about very slowly. Trade associations and various interest groups first seek to digest and explain proposals for legislative change and, once the laws are enacted, to educate their members about the laws' impact. In Russia, however, all these important laws were passed without that kind of support system.

Let me use tax law as an illustration. In 1991, Russia's passage of the first tax law was revolutionary, because previously there was no need for taxation: the state kept everything, then allocated payments. Individual taxes of a minor kind were required but were paid by the employer. The new tax system was intended to serve as a lever to enable the state to achieve modifications in the economy without actually running it. However, the system didn't work because there were too many taxes and the rates were too high and tax collection was unsuccessful. The system is stable now, and major reforms are pending before the Duma that promise to correct the biggest failings of the system.

An equally important fundamental concept, introduced early by Gorbachev and since reinforced by the Constitution and other enactments, is the legal principle of freedom to engage in entrepreneurship, in any business that does not violate public policy. Also introduced under Gorbachev was a law that turned the fundamental rule of contracting on its head. In the Soviet era there was freedom to contract only in regard to defined activities and in accordance with prescribed forms. Now, something akin to our principle is in force: one is free to contract in regard to anything that does not violate the law or public policy.

I would like to comment in greater detail on the impact of the Russian Constitution and the privatization laws on commercial activity. The Constitution ensures the right to engage in business. It provides that each person shall have the right to freely use his abilities and property to engage in entrepreneurial or other economic activity not prohibited by law. That statement is sufficiently clear. The Constitution also provides that no economic activities aimed at monopolization or unfair competition shall be allowed. It further ensures against the retroactive application of laws that create new obligations, and it ensures compensation for damages inflicted by the wrongful action of government agencies or their officials. Those words have tremendous significance for a player in the private economy, and we are beginning to see litigation that calls upon these sections of the Constitution. For example, the Russian bankers' association has filed suit against the Ministry of Finance and other organs of government, challenging the action in August 1998 that froze the ability of banks to pay back their hard-currency loans. The association argues that the government injured its members' relations with foreign lenders and seeks compensation for this wrongful treatment. The suit probably will take several years to wind through the courts, but it is characteristic of the legal actions seen these days.

The Constitution also provides that international treaties and universally acknowledged principles and standards of international law shall be recognized as an integral part of the Russian legal system. This means a great deal for human rights activists. It also means a great deal in a commercial context. If international standards define the way a particular industry or commercial practice should be governed, one can call upon those standards in interpreting Russian law. Further, in the Russian hierarchy of law, international treaties rank higher than Russian legislation, just below the Constitution. In other words, where the commercial world is protected by a host of bilateral and multilateral treaties dealing with matters ranging from tax to intellectual property protection to access to orbital slots, these treaties – if Russia is a signatory – take precedence over national law. From an American perspective – and American lawyers rely on the U.S. Constitution all the time when they are litigating – the Russian Constitution has some unique and reassuring provisions relating to commerce. It remains to be seen how these provisions will be brought into play, but if Russian jurists are as distinguished as their counterparts in the United States, the result will be positive.

Now I would like to comment on the privatization process. Historians, journalists, the idle rich, and countless others will be analyzing the pros and cons of Russia's privatization measures for years to come. Having had practical acquaintance with these historic events, I believe that privatization was a remarkable achievement. As you know, three categories of businesses were involved: small, medium-sized, and large. The first two sectors were privatized very quickly, according to law. The assets of the small businesses were sold off, and the companies collapsed. As for the medium-sized businesses, in most cases the workers, the management, and some outside investors purchased the stock, in accordance with the privatization legislation. No revolution occurred when these companies passed into private hands, because their prior managers continued to manage them. That was the intended result. It was not theft; it was not criminal behavior; it was merely the procedure chosen. Now change is being propelled by the economic crisis, and it is becoming a lever for changing the behavior of many managers.

In the third sector – large businesses – the story is not yet over. Some foolish measures were instituted, like the loans-for-share program, as well as others not so foolish, like the privatization of large companies such as Lukoil. The oligarchs who were the beneficiaries of loans-for-shares are no longer as powerful as they once were; they are struggling to retain their Swiss bank accounts and to keep from losing their major assets in Russia. Their power has been reduced. In some cases, all or parts of the entities they acquired are up for sale again, because of debts owed to creditors as well as tax obligations to the state. Again, a distinction must be drawn: bad laws were adopted by policymakers, but there were few profligate violations of the law. Rather, there was execution of unwise policy.

Today Russia has all manner of guarantees to support commercial activity. It has a highly developed, if formalistic, legal system. A large percentage of business is conducted in accordance with the new rules that are in force, but problems occur when those relationships break down. The court system does not build confidence; neither the courts nor the litigators have the expertise necessary for the system to function effectively. Even in this area, however, there is progress.

Russia's biggest failures in creating a private market economy have resulted not so much from flaws in the laws as from mistakes made by its political leaders and from a deficit of managerial talent. For example, the privatized laws allowed the managers to take over state assets, but they lacked the experience and training required to turn those companies around and stagnation ensued.

In closing, I would like to quote an early twentieth-century writer as a somewhat long-winded way of referring to the need to "genetically code" respect for the law: "It might be said that the Russian people set out very late on their historical path and that we have no need to develop the ideas of individual freedom and personal rights, the rule of law and the constitutional government on our own. Because all these ideas have long since been proclaimed, elaborated in detail and implemented, therefore, we need only borrow them. But even if this were the case, we would still have to live these ideas; however old an idea may be, it is always new for the persons experiencing it for the first time." [3] That is the challenge facing Russia today.

3. Bogden Kistiakovskii, Vekhi, 1909.

PART II

DEVELOPING THE ETHICAL UNDERPINNINGS OF A FREE-MARKET ECONOMY

ADVENTURES OF A RESTAURATEUR

ARKADII NOVIKOV

Arkadii Novikov, a gifted entrepreneur in his late thirties, has created restaurants ranging from fast-food eateries to elegant, high-end establishments in Moscow. All are organized along different thematic lines and reflect his ability to balance entrepreneurial savoir faire, good visual sense, entertainment value, and fine food. A graduate of a Moscow culinary school, Mr. Novikov continues to generate new restaurant concepts. Here he discusses some of the ethical challenges facing businessmen in Russia today.

IN STARTING my businesses, I have faced many kinds of difficulties and challenges. Every businessman in Russia faces the same obstacles today. To make the current situation clear, I would like to give an account of my experiences in the catering sector and the restaurant business after the economic crisis in Russia.

We Russians watch American movies and read American books, and we are familiar with the "American dream." To us that means that a person is able to achieve what he wants, to become rich, to attain high political office. I have been able to realize a Russian version of the American dream during the course of the six years I have spent trying to develop my business. That is what I want to describe here today.

I was born in a very simple Russian family. I lived with my mother and grandmother; my father did not live with us. My mother worked, but her income was tiny, and the three of us lived in a two-room apartment only thirty-six meters square. My bed and my mother's were perpendicular to one another, very close together. Our living accommodations were not what you would call good. Nevertheless, I lived my life, went to high school, and seemed not much different from other teenagers all over the world. I was an average student and

my grades were mostly "Cs." You know how that is: everyone as-
sumes that you're going to be a "C" person; you will remain a "C"
person forever.

After I graduated from high school, I attempted to get into college. Luckily – as things turned out – I was not admitted. In those
days I was extremely thin, and people teased me because of my size.
I was always the smallest and shortest, and people laughed at me.
People also made remarks because of my being Jewish, and I would
fight and then come home with no buttons on my jacket. Well,
everything is different now, and all the buttons are in place. Things
began to change when my mother gave me some advice: "Why
don't you become a cook? At least you'll put on a little weight and
get teased less." The result was a kind of metamorphosis.

I had never been particularly interested in cooking. Gradually,
however, I found that I liked what I was doing, and I had excellent
teachers. I would come home, cut up vegetables, and show my
mother what great potatoes I could make. Then I was called up for
military service. After two years in the Soviet Army, I returned
home and went to work as a cook, preparing meat and other foods
in a plain restaurant. I continued my program of study and specialized in the economics of public catering. I graduated during *perestroika,* a time of change for my country and, as it turned out, for me
as well. Somewhere deep inside, I felt an urge to change and grow.
I worked as a sous chef, then as a head chef for four months. Next
I tried to introduce a menu of my own creation. In the Soviet era,
restaurant patrons often would find that the dish they wanted to order was unavailable. The waiter would simply bring whatever was
on hand, saying "Eat and be silent." So I decided to add a potluck
special to my menu and name it "Eat and be silent." That cost me
my job.

This mishap turned out to be a blessing in disguise, because I
next was given a chance to work in a corporate restaurant. There
I met someone in show business, in the music industry, and he offered me a chance to be chef of a restaurant. Though everything is
good today, those were the most interesting times for me, because

I had a real feeling of freedom. I could cook whatever I wanted, use whatever product I wanted. There was no regulatory organization to check how much butter or how much meat I included in a meal; it was a fascinating experience. Gradually I moved up the ladder and became assistant manager. At that point I realized that I needed even more freedom. By nature I'm an adventurer; I'm probably still an adventurer today. Finally I decided to open my own restaurant.

First, I needed money. I thought that wouldn't be a problem; I'd find the money somehow. Second, I needed a space, so we rented a space from a technical school: my first restaurant. My wife had been abroad, though I hadn't, and I asked her to tell me what restaurants were like in Italy. She described a restaurant that was full of aquariums, so I thought, okay, we'll do something like that in Russia. I met an investor who was in the food business and we spent $50,000 on that first restaurant. It wasn't enough, so I invested some of my own money. I even took my only vacuum cleaner from home to clean the carpets in the restaurant. For about two years the only thing I did was work on expanding the restaurant. Now it is very popular. You can see through the floor, and under it there is a tank of fish. Foreigners love it; it's a fascinating, inviting place. It's a seafood restaurant, naturally, and we have an Italian chef. Before the economic crisis, the restaurant had an income of about $500,000 per month, and we paid between $50,000 and $75,000 in taxes each month.

Then I started my second restaurant, Club T. It was the result of a dream. In general, I approach setting up a restaurant not as a businessman but as an artist; I always want to create a work of art, something very beautiful and unusual. This restaurant features classical French cuisine, and the chef is French. Another division of our company specializes in interior design, and we chose a German firm to design this particular restaurant.

Next, I decided to start a restaurant outside of town, near where Boris Yeltsin lives. Its name is the Tsar's Hunting Lodge, and it is built largely of wood, in the traditional style. It is paradoxical: though *perestroika* had been in progress for five or six years, there was not

Interior of Club T

a single restaurant that featured authentic Russian cuisine. There were Italian, French, German, and other restaurants, but nothing Russian. It is quite popular; even Yeltsin visited us several years ago. In the summer months, the high season, we take in nearly $900,000 a month there. Not many restaurants in Russia or abroad can boast that kind of income.

Our next venture was an Uzbek restaurant, because the cuisine of the Uzbek republic had always been very popular in Russia. It's similar to Moroccan food: pilaf, shish kabob, and the like. It's currently one of my most popular projects. Including the summer area, there are 250 seats; it is fairly large and has a high rate of turnover, yet it still looks comfortable and cozy.

Another restaurant, which features Georgian cuisine, is called White Sun of the Desert. The price for a dinner is comparatively low, in terms of Moscow prices. The restaurant was named for a movie; in fact, its entire theme is based on the movie. The design

Interior of Tsar's Hunting Lodge

of the building combines elements of modern architecture with typical features of a Georgian country interior.

Then there is the Grand Opera Restaurant. I wanted to create a restaurant that would resemble a theater, so we rented space in Moscow's Hotel Budapest. It can seat 120 persons. We will invest a large sum of money in this venture; it was designed for people who want to have a good time and want to spend their money freely. It was built before the crisis, in a period comparable to the New Economic Policy (NEP) era earlier in the twentieth century.

Recently I was named president of the Elki-Palki chain of restaurants. Like everything else in my life, this came about by chance. I had become a "serious businessman," and I had a friend who wasn't really engaged in any activity, so I decided to help him. We rented about 120 square meters of space in a shopping center to

Interior of White Sun of the Desert

Interior of Grand Opera Restaurant

start a small restaurant. Each of us invested $35,000. It quickly became a success, with huge lines and about three or four people for each of the eighty spaces throughout the day, and we decided to open more. It took only three or four months to recoup our investment. Recently, we opened our ninth Elki-Palki.

Before the crisis everything seemed to be going smoothly, and I thought everything we came up with was ingenious. Even though the Elki-Palki prices are not high, the income was $15 million. The restaurants are in good locations and have never relied on loans, so we reinvested some of our profits in development. Most of the restaurants were built with our own money and were operated on a self-financing basis. Maybe that is what saved us when the crisis came, because the organizations that depended on loans went out of business. The main challenge with the Elki-Palki chain is that our principal costs continue to be rent, food, and wages. We did not increase the prices of our meals in proportion to the increase in the dollar exchange rate; we raised them only by a factor of two, despite the soaring exchange rate. We spend a great deal on rent, and this cost is unlikely to decrease. We did not use the crisis as an excuse for massive price hikes – though others did – because our restaurants are geared toward a middle-class clientele and people with modest incomes. For us to survive now, we have to balance the food prices and our costs. In general, however, everything is going fairly well, though our turnover has decreased by about 30 to 40 percent. I hope to develop this chain further, and I hope the economy will grow. Like all other businessmen in Russia, we restaurant owners count our earnings not in rubles, but in dollars, so our proceeds keep dropping.

In conclusion, I want to say that I look forward to a change in Russia's political situation and to seeing more able people taking part in government and passing the right laws. No businessman who operates in Russia can conduct his business honestly. He always has to steal here and there, unpleasant though this word may be. That's what the situation is today: it's virtually impossible to develop business on the basis of current Russian laws. I hope that the new government, when it comes to power, will give normal, genuine opportunities to entrepreneurs, will allow them to develop. Money, after all, is the heart of any economy.

AN EXPLORATION

OF OPTIMISM AND HOPE

JUNIOR ACHIEVEMENT IN RUSSIA

NINA KUZNETSOVA

Nina Kuznetsova is executive director of Junior Achievement (JA) Russia, which now is teaching over one million Russian secondary-school students the fundamentals of market economies and business ethics. Ms. Kuznetsova, who holds a doctoral degree in linguistics from the Pushkin Institute, served as deputy director of the Cross-cultural Communication Department at Moscow International University and as training and development manager of the Cross-cultural and Foreign Language Immersion Programs at Moscow State University's Center for Intensive Foreign Language Instruction. She has also been a consultant to the Russian Diplomatic Academy, the International Monetary Fund, and the International Union of Economists. Under her leadership, JA Russia has become the second largest member of JA International, with forty-two regional centers as of mid-2000.

A Promising Scenario

OF ALL THE CHANGES to sweep the world in recent times, perhaps one of the most profound is the recognition by young people around the globe that market-based economies are effective in delivering economic growth. That change presents one of the greatest growth scenarios in modern history, particularly for youngsters willing and able to take advantage of the opportunity. Since 1991, Junior Achievement Russia has offered programs designed to help that nation's youth make the transition to a market-oriented economy. Now, some 650,000 schoolchildren in forty-one regional centers throughout the Russian Federation, including the remote Sakhalin Islands, have participated in JA's educational programs.[1]

The promising scenario described above has another aspect, of equal importance. As people recognize the merits of private-property ownership and risk-and-rewards relationships and see the benefits of self-reliance and individual initiative, they also need to recognize that this philosophy must be combined with and, if necessary, moderated by respect for the rights and values of others. Successful market-based economies do not tolerate unbridled individualism that involves infringement of the rights of others. Society can function only when the environment is protected and the health and safety of citizens are assured. To make the sound decisions that will create such protection and assurance, people need to be economically literate, and that is the goal toward which JA Russia is striving.

Russia in Transition

What does economic literacy mean in Russia, where the road to a market economy is so painful and rough?

For more than seventy years, the economically literate were those who understood and accepted the roles of the citizens and the state as decreed by Communist political ideology. The government, the mass media, the educational institutions, and the youth organizations reinforced economic interpretations of that ideology. With the

1. Junior Achievement was founded in 1919 by Horace A. Moses, president of the Strathmore Paper Company in Springfield, Massachusetts, on the premise "who better to teach youth about business than business." JA is the oldest and largest not-for-profit global organization of corporate sponsors, business volunteers, teachers, and students engaged in economic and business education. Students are introduced to a variety of business and economic concepts, ranging from the role of business in a global economy to business ethics to commitment to environmental and social issues.

collapse of the Communist regime, Russia rejoined the global community, experiencing all the joys of newly obtained freedom and all the challenges of restructuring society politically and economically. Transition to a market-oriented economy made the functioning of the relatively well-designed and efficient Russian school system, with educational standards that were considered among the world's best, more difficult if not downright impossible. Today Russia is attempting to create a general curriculum that reflects the needs of modern life and meets the rigorous demands of the competitive global marketplace, but the reformers' efforts are hampered by the uncertainty and disorder that surround all efforts at economic and social reform, as well as by the current economic crisis. Despite numerous attempts to reform the Russian school system, the educational process is essentially unchanged; in fact, school performance has deteriorated since efforts at reform began.

Naturally, the educational system reflects all the features of the social and economic environment. Serious obstacles to real and lasting educational reform are rooted in the current economic and political situation: inadequate financial support; conservative attitudes and resistance to change; outmoded management styles based on centralization and bureaucratic methods; and unsatisfactory socialization, characterized by failure to develop values, poor relationships with families and communities, and a gap between education and the realities of the labor market.

As a consequence, Russia's schools now face major difficulties:
- poor condition of plant and equipment; lack of textbooks and program materials
- inability of school administrators to organize and manage the educational process (absence of support from government and local authorities; lack of professional knowledge and skills)
- shortage of highly qualified teachers, many of whom quit because of low pay and delays in payment
- unfavorable changes in professional training and staff upgrading

- low level of teacher qualification; use of old-fashioned teaching techniques
- curriculum that does not prepare students for the demands of modern life or for higher education
- low standards; need for additional, after-school training for those wishing to pass entrance exams at colleges and universities
- lack of training in skills needed for higher-level jobs, which makes many students unemployable
- inadequate programs for gifted and talented students or students with learning difficulties
- lack of motivation, which causes students to leave school early and take low-level jobs
- lack of adult supervision and family care after school
- collapse of the network of extracurricular institutions
- involvement of students in criminal activities, especially among youth from economically disadvantaged families.

Educational decision makers, teachers, students, and parents all are unhappy with the kind of education now provided by Russia's schools. All are convinced that major changes are vital to the country's present and future, and that society and the educational system should provide opportunities for learning, physical education, development of a healthy lifestyle, and cultivation of aesthetic, religious, and moral values, as well as acquisition of the social and economic knowledge and skills necessary to adapt in a changing society.

ja Russia: A Powerful Catalyst

Few would deny that the challenges facing Russia's youth today are different from those faced by their parents' generation, and few would dispute the need for today's youth to learn to function in economic conditions dramatically different from those their parents knew. Currently, the economic and political climate in Russia suggests that without sufficient knowledge of economics and business, the discredited ideas of the past could regain favor. Past influences offer neither a guarantee of future success nor an excuse for failure. As Sir John Templeton put it, "Changes should be seen not as a problem but as a challenge – a form of progress that will lead to better methods of producing results." The wisest course, then, would be to promote development of those skills and attitudes that prepare young people to become creators rather than inheritors.

That ideal has been championed by Junior Achievement for eighty years now. Participants in JA programs learn to see problems as challenges, difficulties as opportunities for success. Therefore JA programs seem well suited to the Russian context, in light of the country's seventy years as a tightly controlled economy in which the concept of market forces was nonexistent. The nonprofit, nongovernment community was the first to accept the new set of challenges, establishing itself as a key player in the introduction of economic and business education to Russia's schools.

Junior Achievement Russia was launched in 1991 with a formal signing ceremony in the Kremlin. It was immediately perceived as a powerful agent for change in the country's transition to a market economy. Since then it has grown rapidly to become the second-largest JA organization in the world, outranked only by the United States.

In 1991, many Western companies were just establishing operations in Russia, and were eager to participate in the emergence of a major market economy. Those companies were willing to contribute to worthy social causes and to be good corporate citizens. JA, fortunately, was viewed as one such worthy cause. Accordingly, generous corporate donations, in combination with a U.S. Agency for International Development (USAID) grant, got JA Russia off to a good start.

The key mission of JA Russia is to catalyze the rapid growth of JA educational programs and experience throughout the country, tailoring these offerings to the national culture and language. To that end, the organization uses advanced teaching methods to provide interesting and inspirational material for teachers and students, relying on the concept of *partnership* between the business community and the educational community. By involving members of the international community, international organizations, corporate sponsors, decision makers, educators, and teachers, the programs deliver important input on economic and social reform, along with high-quality education in the fields of business and economics.

The Network of Support

JA Russia continues to receive invaluable support from such organizations as USAID, the U.S. Information Service (USIS), the International Research and Exchange Board (IREX), Eurasia Foundation, the Center for International Private Enterprise (CIPE), the Ford Foundation, the Citicorp Foundation, and the Chase Manhattan Foundation. In 1998, during a visit to Moscow, First Lady Hillary Rodham Clinton announced a new $1.3 million partnership program between USAID and JA Russia. Under the two-year program, USAID will provide grant funding to ensure the continuation of JA's widely successful market-based educational programs and hands-on business activities for Russian students. That assistance will enrich existing programs, train additional teachers in the use of the JA curriculum, allow at least 350,000 more students to participate, and establish a self-renewing fund to guarantee JA's future sustainability in Russia.

Many major American corporations, too, support the organization: Exxon, Arthur Andersen, Procter & Gamble, Ford Motor Company, Boeing, American Express, Ernst & Young, Citibank, and Reynolds Metals. Their assistance enables JA Russia to develop new educational materials, expand existing ones, and promote advanced teaching techniques; conduct competitions where achievers demonstrate their knowledge and skills; and fund operational activities. Equally important is the investment of executives' energy, effort, and time in support of the curriculum, by applying the principle of "learning by doing." Their involvement demonstrates ethical business conduct in a concrete way and provides an example for future employees to follow.

One unswerving champion of the JA programs is Dr. Evgenii Velikhov, the founding father of Junior Achievement Russia, who believes that they are an essential plank in Russia's reform movement. Another supporter is the Honorable James Collins, the U.S. Ambassador to Russia, whose willingness to open his residence, Spaso House, to JA Russia has been of enormous help. The current chairman of JA Russia's board of directors, George MacDonald, an Exxon Corporation executive, has made himself visible and accessible to students, teachers, and regional directors. His commitment is a powerful example of corporate leadership and good citizenship, as was that of his predecessor, Hans Jochum Horn, managing director of Arthur Andersen. Business leadership of this kind is making an important difference, changing attitudes among a high-impact segment of society: Russia's youth. That is where reform will strike root.

Thus far JA Russia has been unable – with a few notable exceptions – to find a broad and significant base of domestic patrons. Almost all the funds made available for the organization and its work have come from Western agencies, organizations, foundations, and corporations. JA Russia, however, will continue to cultivate domestic patrons and to forge links with the educational establishment. Many members of the educational community already have done an outstanding job in adapting JA programs to Russian circumstances and pedagogical traditions. The critical ingredient of the organization's success is that its programs have become truly indigenous.

Current Programs and Goals

JA Russia continues to reach out to the more traditional educational establishment, especially in regions where Communist influence is relatively strong. Some educators protest what they see as the foreign content of JA's programs and methods. This situation results primarily from competition among different organizations and individual authors seeking to win contracts for textbooks and seminars in the field of economics. Other educators welcome the introduction of progressive elements into the Russian context, but worry about the disharmony between the idealized image of the world of business and market relations and the actual conditions of the Russian economy, including the highly unstable nature of Russian capitalism, with its links to organized crime. Hundreds of thousands of Russian students respond to those concerns with their huge demand for JA programs, where they learn that doing business ethically makes much more sense.

The programs benefit students and teachers alike. Russian teachers who work with the JA curriculum demonstrate increased self-esteem and tolerance, an ability to teach interactively, and show more respect for and interest in their students' opinions. The courses include formal lessons, role playing, computer simulations, classroom debates, case studies, creation of mock companies, and a wide variety of extracurricular assignments. Funding from the business community and foundations allows the programs to be provided at little or no cost to schools and students.

Despite the record of success, the goal of real economic literacy has not yet been achieved; the hard work of reforming the teaching of economics in Russia's schools is not over. All JA's efforts are now threatened in the increasingly conservative cultural and financial climate. Moreover, some unscrupulous authors and organizations seek to take advantage of the popularity of JA Russia's teaching materials and methods, without appropriate regard for the organization's logo and copyright.

A further difficulty is the challenge of building a network of regional centers that work in different financial, political, and cultural environments. Efforts to make the regional centers self-financing are complicated by financial and logistical obstacles, as well as by the inability of centers and JA teachers to pay dues or membership fees, to establish local boards in most cases, and to gain the support of local business. JA programs have been launched in eighty of the eighty-nine regions of the Russian Federation, but with appropriate financial support the number of centers could be increased. The demand for the programs is impressive and hard to satisfy; it is limited by scarce financial resources and the unavailability of dedicated members of local business communities.

It is worth examining some of the programs in greater detail. "Seven Steps into the World of Economics" is designed for students from six through twelve years of age. It answers basic questions such as What is a business? How does a community work? and What's the difference between a need and a want? These are the seven steps: "Ourselves," "Our Families," "Our Community," "Our City," "Our Region," "Our Nation," and "Our World."

"Next Step," the program for middle school students, teaches skills ranging from planning a budget to managing a business. It combines practical, hands-on learning with theory-based curriculum. Scheduled for implementation in 2000 are a variety of segments dealing with economic issues: "Personal Economics," "Enterprise in Action," "The International Marketplace," and "The Economics of Staying in School."

"Applied Economics," introduced in 1992, is a program for high school students in Russian general educational institutions such as secondary schools, lyceums, and specialized schools. Its theoretical part includes a textbook, a study guide, and MESE (Management Economic Simulation Exercise) software. Macroland, its practical part, gives students a chance to operate their own company. In teams of five, they learn to organize an enterprise, produce and sell a product, offer services, keep records, and analyze financial activities. Their work culminates in a series of Student Company Trade Fairs, and the winners of regional events compete in the National Student Company Rally for the title of "Best Student Company of the Year." Thanks to generous support from Exxon and the administration of the Radisson-Slavianskaia Hotel, more than 150 of the best students from Russia's regions convene in Moscow to participate in the event annually.

At the competition, student companies display and trade their products and services. The most common products are leather goods, woodcrafts, painted plaques and boxes, Easter eggs, beaded jewelry, and knitted hats. The most popular services include editing, printing, computer typesetting, running on-line school newspapers, designing web pages, and holding lotteries and disco parties. Guests and visitors have a chance to talk with young entrepreneurs and to learn about and purchase their products and services while the jury evaluates the work of the student businesses. The best companies receive the JA Russia Diploma, as well as prizes provided by the rally's general sponsor, Exxon Corporation. The annual rallies are followed by an evening reception hosted by U.S. Ambassador James Collins.

Since 1992, JA Russia has conducted annual national telecommunications Management Economic Simulation Exercise (MESE) competitions for high school students from various regions of Russia in JA's Applied Economics program. The MESE National Cup in Moscow has been sponsored by Hewlett-Packard since 1996.

The real highlight of Junior Achievement Russia is the JA students themselves. Russian achievers have excelled in international student competitions such as the Hewlett-Packard Global Business Challenge (HPGBC), where students from around the world compete against each other as managers of computer-simulated businesses. During this multi-week event, students make decisions affecting the price, production, marketing, and distribution of a fictional product. The decisions are sent via e-mail to a processing center in the United States. The teams with the best strategy advance to a final championship round. Since 1996, the year the HPGBC began, Russian teams have won first place.

More innovative instructional approaches are being planned. JA Russia is now working on a computer-driven banking simulation called Banks in Action. The new project will train 3,200 JA teachers and reach 131,000 high school students over a two-year period. It highlights the fundamental role banks play in a market economy and entails competitive student interaction led by volunteers familiar with bank operations. Banks in Action is funded by IREX and the Citicorp Foundation.

Since 1995, JA Russia has been a member of Young Enterprise Europe (YEE). This association unites national organizations with the common purpose of enabling young people to learn more about the world through the real experience of running their companies, supported by volunteers from the business community. JA Russia takes part in all YEE annual events, including the European Student Company Competition and the European Trade Fair and Congress. In 2001, JA Russia will host the Student Company Competitions.

For several years, JA Russia has offered special programs to provide students with recreation and education during their vacations. The regional centers, supported by members of the national staff, have set up special economic centers at recreation facilities. The programs are designed to familiarize students with advanced micro- and macroeconomics, as well as to give them practical experience in organizing and operating state institutions and private enterprises. Participants simulate a state model in accordance with current economic and legal reality, following ethical principles. As they elect a government, create a federal bank, tax authority, accounting and audit services, a commodities and stock exchange, and employment agencies, they learn more about economics, understand basic financial operations, become familiar with the principles of taxation, and acquire other useful skills.

Challenges for the Future

All these programs, of course, require a great deal of support, as USAID recognized when it awarded JA Russia a grant to rejuvenate and expand its offerings. The grant coincided with the beginning of the academic year – and with Russia's financial crisis. Now, JA Russia is able to administer the funds prudently and show results. We are fortunate to have such support, and we will continue to seek funds for projects and operations.

As a not-for-profit organization, JA normally relies heavily on corporate contributions to fund its educational programs and the associated administrative costs. In recent months, however, the economic and political climate in Russia has turned decidedly sour. Many Western companies are struggling to be profitable, and some are leaving the country. Today, business prospects seem bleak for most companies, and contribution budgets have been substantially reduced or eliminated. Ironically, this is happening just when JA programs are needed most. The political will to reform seems weak. The young people of Russia have had a look at the way a market economy functions, however, and they are eager to learn more. The JA programs are ideally suited to this situation.

Russia is a challenge for JA; of that there can be no doubt. At the same time, there is an enormous market with all the ingredients for success: an enthusiastic population of young people in an emerging market economy; highly respected JA champions who are proven believers and doers; educators who support and encourage; a motivated corps of professional teachers and administrators; programs tailored to the national culture and language; generous international aid; and a national tradition of learning, adapting, and succeeding. Russia has what it takes to succeed!

SMALL BUSINESS IN RUSSIA

A VIEW FROM UNDER THE TABLE

LEONID V. IVANOV

Leonid Ivanov is president and founder of Klever Group, Inc., a software and Internet company with offices in Moscow, California, and Germany. Here he provides a comparative perspective based on his experiences in setting up business operations in the West and gives insight into general structural problems of business ethics in Russia in a larger sense.

I look at the world from under the table.
The twentieth century is an unusual century:
The more interesting an epoch is to a historian,
The sadder it is to a contemporary.
– Nikolai Glazkov

THIS CHAPTER is not precisely a "report from the front." Things in Russia are changing so rapidly that the adverb "now" can scarcely apply with any accuracy. Instead, I will examine trends that I think are profound enough to persist and exert influence for some time. I apologize if my remarks occasionally seem too radical and subjective. But hasn't it been the historical role of Russians to be subjective and radical – and to apologize for it later?

I would like to compare my company's Russian experience with its experience in the United States. Eleven years ago, when we started our software business in Moscow, it was among the country's first new enterprises. Until then I had thought of leaving Russia to start the business, but just at that time the government began allowing people to own and operate their own small enterprises, so I stayed.

The Beginning

One of the first things I noticed about doing business in Russia was how little people actually knew about business. They almost seemed to be implementing the notions of capitalism that had been taught to us in school. We were told, for example, that in the West, businessmen are ready to kill their competitors over a dollar, and Russian businessmen started doing just that.

Another important issue in Russia was the obtaining of start-up capital. Since ours was one of the first new businesses, I found myself advising many would-be entrepreneurs. Later I met one of them again, now famous and a multimillionaire, and he expressed his gratitude for everything I had told him that night eight years ago. When I asked why – I had forgotten our talk – he said, "You told me how important it is to be honest. You said it really does matter how one obtains start-up capital. So when I left your office" – which in reality was my apartment – "I realized that I should do exactly the opposite, that I should steal and do anything I could to get my first $100,000. And then I would become honest. And here I am today."

Another interesting phenomenon was the general public's attitude toward businessmen. At first they were perceived as freedom fighters, hero-dissidents of a sort. Later, when their primary concern turned out to be profit, not the common good, disillusion set in, and businessmen became one of the most hated groups in the public eye.

My company's first product was a database of Russian legislation. Over our eleven-year history we have worked with all sorts of government offices as official partners in the maintenance of the database. One of the first was the Arbitration Court of the Soviet Chamber of Commerce and Industry. One day I met with an official of this court, and he looked frightened. He said, "I have just learned that there is a similar product."

"So what," I replied, "there is nothing wrong with competition." I told him that on a visit to West Germany I had seen three gas sta-

tions at one intersection, for example, and they were seemingly doing fine.

"No!" he said, "That is not what the product should be. I want
people standing in line in front of my office; I want them begging
for our product; I want them to give my secretary candies and per-
fumes in order to get it. That is what a good business product
should be."

In all honesty I have to say that this attitude is not limited by geography. In California we are dealing with a communications company that holds a monopoly in our area, and it has acquired all the
attributes of a Soviet-style organization.[1] Other businesses that deal
with them have become frustrated, as I was until I remembered my
Soviet experience; then it all worked out fairly well. In Russia, when
left no choice but to deal with a terrible service, you try to find
someone nice within the organization. Later, when everyone else is
in trouble, you will still be okay. These tactics worked in Russia, and
they work in America when you are forced to deal with a company
that offers unsatisfactory service. It is a human phenomenon, not

---

1. I recall meeting with our first account representative, who was wearing old
jeans and a dirty T-shirt. His hair was dyed pink and orange, and his behavior was
godlike. He had a habit of telling one company bad things about another. He
would say, for example, "I don't like Company X, so I have decided it shouldn't stay
in business in the area." Luckily, he was promoted. This company bills its customers about twice what they actually owe, and it is impossible to fight the incor-
rect charges. At the same time, you can't afford to have the company disconnect
your service: You'd lose all your business. You end up owing $60,000 on paper –
so everyone is guilty of sitting still and trying not to complain. Nobody tries to sell
you anything; you have to beg for service and, if you are lucky, you will get it six
months later. If you call the rep or the technical support person, your call will be
returned a month later. Meanwhile, this company can afford to permit constant
service interruptions, because nobody is willing to complain. Another typical
Soviet-style feature: Small businesses and large businesses are treated differently.
Often, when service goes down, the company says that one of the larger companies it hosts took all the bandwidth, and it believes that this is a legitimate
explanation.

a specifically Russian one. It is easier to observe and analyze in the Russian setting, however, because Russian business is still in its infancy, in a laboratory state.

Business Ethics

Business ethics cannot be separated from the ethics of society. One problem in Russia is the idea of "us" and "them." A country is doing best, I believe, when its people consider the majority of their countrymen as "us." I experienced this feeling in Moscow during the 1991 coup, and it was wonderful! Recently I talked to a hardcore liberal who said how good it was that the government was cleansing Moscow of people from the Caucasus, "because they have a different culture; they steal, they rape, they kill." I thought to myself, if the same were said of the Jews, he would be up in arms. During the most recent elections being held in California, my manager, a very conservative man who usually votes for "anything Republican that moves," told me, "I voted for Democrats for all the positions that had to do with social issues. I want Republicans to handle my money, but Democrats to handle my retirement." My dream is that Russians will someday take a similar approach, with everyone able to admit that his opponent wishes the country well, but just expresses it differently.

I first expected prices and labor costs to be relatively low in Russia. That definitely was not the case. Moreover, I discovered that it was often cheaper to hire someone in the United States than in Russia to do the same job. Many business-related services are cheaper in the United States. To analyze this situation thoroughly would require a separate paper; I merely want to note it here as one of the impediments to the development of small business in Russia. One possible contributing factor may be that in Russia – at least in Moscow, the city I know best – many people were left with substantial and valuable assets, such as apartments, after the collapse of the Soviet system of government. A person there may consider himself very poor because he earns $30 a month, but at the same time he owns a studio apartment worth more than $25,000.

In any event, while the existence of a middle class in Russia is hotly debated, I have to say that I have not noticed any "middle-class" concepts of net worth. There is either "a lot of money" or "no money." In general, many of these problems may derive from a different concept of time. The dominant feeling among Russians is "I want money now, not ten years from now." In general, Russia has a long-standing problem with temporal concepts, as Petr Chadaev, a nineteenth-century philosopher, noted: "Russia has no history, only geography." In terms of business ethics, such attitudes make it hard to conduct any business that is time-dependent (as is most of the business with which I am familiar!). When investing money to obtain higher interest became popular in the late 1990s, nobody repaid loans on time. People were divided into two groups: the honest ones, who paid two years late, and the dishonest ones, who just disappeared.

Most Americans appear to believe that the majority of their countrymen are decent, and this notion reveals yet another area of cultural difference. Any Russian doing business in the United States notices how many things are based on trust. Questionnaire items such as "Have you ever used drugs? Yes/No" are shocking to people with a Russian background. To make the situation even worse, such forms usually explain in fine print that answering "yes" to any of the questions makes you ineligible for consideration. Russia, however, is not the only country where a difference exists. Germany, too, where we also have an office, could benefit from some of the basic presumption of innocence that people enjoy in the United States.

Business Law and the Social Contract

I think it is the government's responsibility to make clear all the rules and regulations of the law. And to be clear, they have to be short.

In 1992, a group of prominent Russian economists wrote "The Liberal Charter," the prototype of a new constitution. One of the articles, later deleted, struck me as naive but true in part. It stated that the body of law restricting citizens' rights should never exceed 1.2 megabytes, the standard capacity of the 5.25-inch floppy disk at that time. This was an effort to ensure that the government could not pass new laws restricting rights without abolishing some of the previous restrictions.

Another problem is that Russian law is constantly changing. The first law regulating private business, the law "On Cooperatives," stated that it would remain in effect in all its parts, including the taxation section, for some time: five years, as I recall. During the next year, over fifty changes were made in it! Not uncommonly, the government enacts legislation and applies it retroactively, so that citizens end up owing back taxes, for example.

I also believe that the law has to be susceptible of execution. On numerous occasions, while working with Russian government officials, we have suggested creating a body that would test new laws through a "model-citizen approach": Can you obey all the rules and still survive? It is a very simple test: Can you drive from any point A to any point B without breaking traffic laws, for example. In Moscow, I don't think you can. The inevitability of such violations creates a situation in which *everyone* is guilty to some extent. A preferential policy is the automatic result, and some people become more equal than others.

Then there arises the issue of the social contract. Surely, no law can work unless the majority of the citizens understand and accept it. A typical example is a law regulating the speed limit. Even in America, it is hard to make people accept a speed limit when they know that the neighboring state has set a different limit. I suspect that organized crime flourishes in periods of history when certain laws do not gain public acceptance and the social contract thus is weakened, as was the case during the Prohibition era in the United States.

Criminal Inclinations

One noticeable thing about Russia is the pervasiveness of crime. I remember how the thin line between right and wrong shifted, slowly but surely, toward the wrong. Ten years ago a partner of mine wanted to exchange rubles for dollars. Such an exchange was illegal at the time, and I found his suggestion so outrageous and dirty that I stopped dealing with him. Now you can change money on every street corner. Most of the businessmen I know think that there remain only two things you should not sell: drugs and weapons. I may be exaggerating a bit here, but only to make my point: criminal behavior and attitudes have thoroughly penetrated life in Russia, including the country's business sector.

Three years ago I met with a prominent American senator, who asked me if there were any honest people in the Russian government, people who wanted to do more than just improve their own well-being. I said that there definitely were such people, that I knew them and worked with them. In fact, we needed government contacts badly for our database on Russian legislation, but we never had enough money for bribes – so I knew for certain that the officials in various government departments who cooperated with us were not doing so for money. The senator asked me to compile a list of honest people; he said he and his colleagues would be interested in working with them. I put together a list of about fifty names, including members of main government bodies such as the State Duma and police officers who were serious about fighting crime. Before faxing the list to the senator, I decided to ask the permission of everyone on it. To my astonishment, they all refused categorically, saying they would lose their jobs if their colleagues learned that they were honest and, moreover, were receiving the approval of Americans. I ended up with an empty list, and I never called the senator again. I felt terrible; something was deeply wrong if honest people were afraid to let their honesty be publicly known.

By contrast, people are not at all reluctant to advertise their connection to the KGB or to organized crime; in fact, they seem rather proud of it. In some offices a portrait of Feliks Dzerzhinsky, the founder of the KGB, hangs openly. Just imagine what an uproar would ensue in Germany if someone were to hang Himmler's portrait in his office! In my opinion, crime has assumed the role formerly played by the Communist Party and its departments such as the KGB. The roots of every organized crime conglomerate in Russia can be traced back to the Party, the Komsomol (the Communist youth organization), and the KGB.

My own story shows how much influence those people once exerted on the life of ordinary Russians. After graduating from the university, I had my first job interview in one of the research institutes of the Academy of Sciences. The department head who interviewed me called later to say that things had gone well and that I was hired. A week later he asked to see me in private. He looked scared. He said that the director of the institute, a man I had never met, told him I was not politically acceptable. The KGB objected to my hiring, he claimed, because of my family. And that happened in 1986! Later the department head who wanted to hire me became the president of one of the republics fighting to gain independence. And in an even more interesting twist, the KGB director who opposed my hiring later became a prime minister of Russia.

Soviet society was much more stratified than Russian society today. People who were powerful and rich had no interest in dealing with the intelligentsia, for example, but new times have created new chains of relationships. Everyone in Russia today is concerned about money. An honest person may invest money in another honest person's business. The second person may loan money to a third party, a thief. In this chain of relationships, only the thief is technically dishonest. The person in the middle, however, inasmuch as he acted as broker, still became an unwilling participant in the crime of theft. The first and second members of the chain can still discuss Plato and Rozanov. The second and third probably would never have met in former times. The honest second person, the one in the middle who reads Plato but still deals with the thief, represents a new social type that has emerged within the past decade. I like this type. His only problem is that the fantasy world in which everyone behaves decently is still more real to him than the world in which he actually lives.

Occurrences of that kind were common in the 1990s, and so far Russian society has not developed a good ethical model to handle them. The tremendous ethical and moral dislocation of our entire society, oddly enough, can be described in terms of the Marxist view of history. We were taught that in history there first existed a highly centralized slave-owning society, much like the Soviet system under Stalin. That society was replaced by a feudal one, with a great number of relatively weak vassals in whose lands organized intimidation and racketeering held sway. This description fits some aspects of modern Russian society, in which criminal groups control certain territories and collect fees from businesses there.[2] Much of this may be a byproduct of the reforms. At some point the government was simply trying to transfer property to as many owners as possible, regardless of who they were, and hoping that the mechanisms of the market would accomplish the rest. According to the Marxist model, the next step is capitalism with its heartless exploitation of workers. It goes hand in hand with technology, allegedly. I hope it will come soon.

Recommendations

To move forward, not solely in economic terms, it is crucial for Russian society first to clearly define crime, then to marginalize it.

2. Many experts argue that it is better – not just in Russia, but also in Latin America, say – to have a few well-organized crime cartels than a host of smaller groups and independent criminals. They believe that the large cartels are easier to manage and rich enough to control street crime and protect their investments. I think, however, and my Russian experience supports this, that the government still can fight crime when there are many smaller groups. When there are a few large groups, they *are* the government.

99

Much of what is happening in Russia now is determined by the fact that membership in organizations such as the Communist Party and the KGB never was officially and clearly labeled as criminal. I am not suggesting that such crime should be followed by punishment, although – just as in Nazi Germany – every member of the established party and the state security police was committing a crime, in my opinion. However, I see no need for show trials or any other kinds of trials. But by not defining such behavior as criminal, we are not giving society a model of what we consider decent and what we consider deplorable. Rather than political show trials designed to impress the public, I would like to see precedent-setting civil litigation against those who committed criminal acts under the old system. The American courts have demonstrated experience with adjudicating the criminal behavior of organizations without limiting freedom of speech, in the Southern Poverty Law Center's suits against the KKK, for example. The United States could also underline the significance of such litigation by allowing the Alien Tort Claims Act to be used against former Communist and KGB officials, instead of inviting them to lecture in American universities. That would not be hard; after all, the ultimate goal of every Russian criminal – whether he be a street-gang leader, a big city mayor, or both – is to have a nice piece of property abroad.

The United States and Russia

Speaking of American-Russian relations and American aid to Russia, I want to mention one more thing. People in America say repeatedly that the United States has won the Cold War and that this victory was achieved by the Reagan administration. Both assertions are wrong, I believe. First, Russia still has a military force of more than one million soldiers and still possesses nuclear weaponry. What has changed over the past decade, however, is Russians' attitude toward the United States. Much of that change is due to American policies toward Russia. Communism collapsed because most Russians wanted it to do so. Each person had his own reasons, but they had nothing to do with Ronald Reagan. If any American president deserves credit for the collapse, it is Jimmy Carter, whose firm stand on human rights and on Afghanistan was noted in Russia. Reagan was ridiculed in our country. He was too similar to our leaders in appearance and behavior; he mixed up the names of countries; he used meaningless slogans like the "Evil Empire." For his Soviet counterparts Reagan made an ideal target; he was everything they wanted an American leader to be. It was the Russians who won their own Cold War against their own corrupt government. But succeeding American administrations did nothing to support Russia, most of the Russian people felt. I never heard of any American government program of assistance, and we all were well aware of assistance from the German government and others.[3]

All we got from the United States was the humiliation we had to swallow in the American Embassy in order to get a visa. We also knew that every famous Russian criminal/businessman was able to get a green card. But no one who grew up here can imagine the terrible trauma of our first impression of the United States. We began to think that the Americans were trying to select only the meanest Russians, people who were ready to lie and push others away in order to get ahead. Nobody ever told us that it was just the U.S. Immigration and Naturalization Service, whose job it was in the twentieth century to forbid entry to anyone who is really decent and in need of help. During Hitler's years in power, more Germans than Jews received American visas. Right now I know of people in Russia who, alleging discrimination, first obtain American refugee status, then prolong that status to stay in Russia for more than a year. Need I continue?[4]

3. American aid programs and organizations would be potential prospects for our Russian legal database, so I think I would have known if they had played a significant role in Russia. I certainly would have tried to contact them to sell our product. Russians were well aware of help provided by Western European countries.

4. I still keep a letter from a vice-consul at the American Embassy in Moscow, claiming that I committed fraud because I married an American citizen two weeks, instead of three, after entering the country. Her allegation was later dismissed as ridiculous, but my sense of humiliation still remained. Our company's vice-

The administrations that followed Carter supported certain people, not issues. They never took a firm stand on any issue. They supported Yeltsin, regardless of his actions. They were not inclined to support ordinary individuals or businesses, only corrupt politicians and government institutes. What if the phone companies, the banks, the HMOs, and scam artists were all you knew about America? What if you had to go through the DMV in order to be admitted to Disneyland? That is similar to the impression we have. What, then, has been achieved since 1980? By withholding assistance and refusing to support important issues, the West led many Russians to believe that they had made the wrong choice. The only real difference is that 75 percent of all Russians now are anti-American. If any American administration will accept the credit for that, I will gladly bestow it.

The Future

What about the future, then, and is there any hope? I think Russia definitely has a future, and there definitely is hope. During our second year at the university, in a course on medieval Russian, we were studying a Smolensk treaty of 1229. Our teacher, Professor Zalizniak, drew our attention to a clause in this treaty that I will provide here in Old Russian and then translate:

> "Урядили пак мир како было любо руси и всему латинескому языку кто то у русе гостит. На том миру аж бы мир тверд был тако был князю любо и рижанам всем и всему латинескому языку. И всем тем кто на оустоко моря ходят. аж бы налезл правду."

> "So they have established this treaty in the way that would be good for Russia, and for all Catholic people who do business in Russia.

---

president for technology just went to the U.S. Embassy to get the necessary forms for obtaining a visa, and now he categorically refuses to travel to the United States because the embassy routine is too degrading.

As long as the treaty will be honored in the way it pleases the prince, and all citizens of Riga and all Catholic people and everyone who goes to the Baltic Sea. Everywhere you can find law."

What our professor explained to us was that in the minds of thirteenth-century Russians, the entire world was divided into parts where you could "find law" – in other words, go to a local sovereign and get a fair trial even if you were a foreigner – and parts where you could not. I hope that some parts of Russia one day will become places where you can actually "find law."

Business is about making predictions for the future. But in eleven years of doing business, I have found that no matter how many options you analyze, no matter how many predictions you make, real life comes up with totally unexpected solutions and versions far more brilliant than those that were in the business plan. In general, and especially where Russia is concerned, history is smarter than we are. And upon that belief I base my hope and optimism for Russia's future. The problem is that there is one thing you should never ask about Russia, whose people have their own notion of time, and that is "When?"

PART III

BUILDING A CIVIL SOCIETY

NURTURING A CHERISHED GARDEN

THE GROWTH OF A YOUTH COMMUNITY

SISTER MARIA BORISOVA

Sister Maria became a nun in 1994, after a career as a chemist in science and industry. She threw all of her considerable talent and energy into church work in 1991, organizing a church school, a youth community, one of the largest scout troops in Russia, and activities ranging from icon painting to church singing to the study of church history. Her personal example illustrates how civil society can be built in a religious context.

A Little Bit About Myself

MY LIFE is interesting only inasmuch as it is typical of Russians of my generation. I will say outright that I am a patriot of my time; I am inexpressibly grateful to God for the opportunity to experience not through reading, nor through the imagination, but in the actual flesh the fulfillment of the ancient Chinese curse (or perhaps blessing): "May you live in an age of changes." I love change; I love strong impressions. I spent my entire youth in the mountains. Hiking was the only safety valve for the youth of my generation, our only illusion of freedom.

My parents were Communists. My mother especially enjoyed anti-religious propaganda, and most of her speeches were tried out on me – not in the interest of propaganda, but for practice. This was an interesting phenomenon: anti-religious propaganda in a country that was almost entirely atheist. Books were published, talks given. So we had at least some source of information on religion. Feeling ashamed of ourselves and not comprehending, with our hearts in our mouths we read "The Comical Bible," "The Comical

Gospels," and the journal *Science and Religion*. But there such words resounded, even though in fragmentary quotations and presented with mockery! Once I even helped my mother write a paper on Christian psychology – based on the novels of Zola. Twenty years later Christian psychology became my profession and my destiny.

I never was what was called a dissident. Kazan' is not Moscow or Saint Petersburg, and in our town almost no one had heard about dissidents. I always avoided public duties, but only because I was ashamed to speak high-flown words about something I didn't believe. Not for worlds would I have joined the Party, but only because I profoundly disliked all the Communists I knew. I couldn't permit myself to be found in their company. But I never doubted for a moment that our system was the best.

My life's program was simple and understandable, like that of all boys and girls "from good families": school graduation with a medal for achievement; university; graduate school; dissertation. Somewhere in the middle of it all, marriage and a child. The problems began when the program was approaching an end, before I had reached the age of thirty. Perhaps if I had been at a more serious scientific center, among really fanatical scholars, my enthusiasm for "major science" would have continued for some time. But I was almost thirty, and I couldn't deceive myself any longer. No discoveries were foreseen; ahead there lay only a career and a materially secure old age. That was too little to live for.

The official registration of my dissertation and the celebration banquet required money, and my salary was insufficient, so I arranged to work as a cleaning woman. That was the first "nonstandard" step in my life. And it was this very action that upset the smooth routine of my destiny. In the place where I cleaned floors, a young man whom I found very strange worked as the watchman. He was a hippie and a believer. Thus I became acquainted with Kazan's hippies, my first youth community. The kids were much younger than I, by eight to ten years; perhaps that is why our hippie group was somewhat unusual. It seemed to me that I was learning from them: internal freedom and figurative, nonstandard thinking. For a long time I didn't see my own influence on their fellowship, and I was not quick to find out that among ordinary hippies, both drugs and "free love" were accepted. We were ascetics and philosophers. This was an extraordinarily Russian version of hippie life – endless nighttime conversations about the destiny of mankind in a smoke-filled four-meter-square "Khrushchev" kitchen.[1] Various strange people from all over the country would come, spend one or two days with us, and leave feeling terribly proud: we were precisely the kind of hippies they had dreamed of. The fame of the "Kazan' *tusovka*" [2] spread not only throughout Russia. At the same time, my scientific career was taking its course. I became a senior research worker and had a part in an interesting invention connected with the manufacture of photographic film. But I was no longer absorbed by the work.

Naturally, this could not continue for long. I began to be summoned to the KGB. At first this was even amusing. After a few polite conversations about nothing, an outspoken recruiting effort began. I had to throw off the mask of a naive little dummy and refuse openly, even rudely. Saying good-bye, they threatened me vaguely. But I announced that I would come to the next meeting only in handcuffs and that in no way would I promise to keep all their conversations secret. Evidently, that was not part of their rules of the game.

Six months later an article appeared in one of the Kazan' newspapers, saying who was hiding behind the mask of a respectable scholar. They were expecting my colleagues to recoil from me in horror, but they hadn't taken my chatterbox nature into account. I had not hidden my "long-haired friends" from anyone. My colleagues rose to my defense – and a scandal broke out. We were summoned to meetings of our institute and to the public prosecu-

---

1. Khrushchev ordered the construction of four- and five-story apartment buildings all over the Soviet Union. These apartments, known as *khrushchevki*, had tiny kitchens no more than five meters square.

2. This word, coined in the 1980s, denotes a kind of rap session, a regular gathering where people would "hang out" and have informal conversation.

tor's office; every day we came home from sessions with the police. An entire commission was formed to investigate me. However entertaining the process may have been, they failed to come up with anything that way either. Now I'm very glad about this entire incident. It gives me a feeling of being involved in this epoch of history. As a matter of fact, everything sorted itself out; I felt only a few keen sensations, not even fear. After all, it was already 1986. I didn't understand right away that two or three years earlier they would have put me into prison for certain, but I'm always lucky. A smart, fearless woman reporter turned up, and six months later, by March 8, an article in my defense appeared in another paper. And the entire incident was over. I was even asked to join the Party *raion* committee, and they tried to assign me to work with youth.

About that time our group of hippies also dispersed little by little. Somehow simultaneously all of us settled down and started families, and soon I too got married. Although dispersed, the groups in our building did not become extinct. We constructed and demolished philosophical systems daily; it was a kind of fireworks display of ideas and fantasies. *Perestroika* was at its height; it was a fascinating time. It seemed that layer by layer the scales were falling from our eyes. Today it is fashionable to say all kinds of awful things about Gorbachev, but I will always be grateful to him for that time of liberation and continuous discovery.

Finally *samizdat* made its way even to Kazan'. I was able to buy heaps of all kinds of books, mainly books on philosophy, because there was a lot of money: the department in which I worked had been converted into a commercial firm, and it began to flourish. But soon philosophy bored us. Philosophical systems began to seem very arbitrary: artificial worlds built according to made-up rules. And out of the entire heap of books, a small group of authors stood out: Berdiaev, Solov'ev, Florenskii – Christian philosophers. Their systems were not so stifling and closed as the others; out of them there led a road to somewhere. And that is how we became interested in Christianity.

Work in the Church and the Creation of a School

In fall 1988, my husband and I were baptized, and immediately we began going to Optina Abbey, where the relics of St. Ambrose of Optina had just been found and a monastery had been opened. At Optina we met a very fine and thoughtful priest, and our spiritual life began. A year later, getting ready for a pilgrimage to Diveev Monastery, we asked our Kazan' *Vladyka*[3] for his blessing on our journey. He rejoiced in us. In those days there were only old ladies in Kazan's churches, and this had greatly depressed him. He suggested that we turn to work in the church, and he became our confessor and spiritual director.

The issue was complicated. My husband liked his work as a programmer, and at that time I was earning a great deal. But, as we repeatedly became convinced later on, everything happens in accordance with the word of our *Vladyka*. Soon thereafter my husband was laid off, and we started to set up a Sunday school for children at the cathedral. There were neither books nor educational aids there. Some things were sent to us from France and some from America. No one had experience of any kind, neither spiritual nor teaching experience. But, at the very least, things got done. After a few months I decided to leave my prosperous firm: business trips were interfering with my teaching. At first I worked as a cook in the diocesan administration, but the work was too much for me. My overweening pride interfered; the transition from science to the kitchen was too abrupt. Soon I was transferred to the cathedral to sell candles and icons. But on Sundays we taught.

For a long time the school suffered because of the lack of decent premises. We had only two classrooms: one was in the bell tower, to which a narrow, steep, extraordinarily bizarre staircase led; the other was in a small, half-tumbled-down shed behind the garbage

3. Title of or mode of addressing a bishop, archbishop, or metropolitan in the Orthodox Church.

bins. The shed's roof leaked constantly, and in winter the icicles hung all the way down to the ground at the entrance. We quickly noticed that after Christmas the number of children in school sharply decreased: their parents got tired of waiting outdoors for them. We started to get the parents involved, and attendance improved.

After several years we encountered yet another problem, which both gladdened and slightly perplexed us. Both the children and the parents refused to graduate from Sunday school and, when the course ended, demanded a continuation. We had to introduce new disciplines into the program. For the adults we started teaching general church history and the history of the Orthodox Russian Church. After a couple of years we added a series of lectures on interpretation of the Gospels and the Psalter. For the children we created a group for studying iconography, including icon painting, and to the course on the Scriptures we added instruction in Old Church Slavonic, the Gospels, and the basis of the liturgy. The school grew quickly, and we were joined by another teacher, a young woman with an outstanding talent for teaching. A library began to be gathered together. From all our trips we dragged back huge packages of books to Kazan'.

My husband at that time spent more and more time in monasteries, and we decided to part. After some time I decided to become a nun. It is difficult to say what led me to that decision. There were naive feelings of exaltation, of course, as well as some fantastic expectations of internal changes. But, as they say, one cannot begin a new life, one can only continue one's life in a new way. Life as a nun has not changed me much. I still love freedom and sharp impressions. Now, truly, I have them in spades. I still love creative work more than anything else in the world. Now my work is more creative and freer than it ever was before. In the person of the *Vladyka* I obtained not only a spiritual director, but also the "administrator of my dreams." All my life my initiative had been hindered by others, people who clumsily organized and skillfully ruined my work. I would not trade our *Vladyka's* respectful interest in our work and his careful, delicate politics of noninterference for any amount of protection or material support. The school has grown like a cherished garden, rather than being built like a brick building.

The Youth Community

Among the adult Sunday school pupils there began to appear more and more students who were no longer children and not yet parents. It was necessary to interact with them somewhat differently; we began to teach them separately from the parents. That was how our youth community began. At first, every year two or three students would join our group, then the number swiftly increased. We perceived that those values that today are presented to youth as priority goals – material benefits and sensual pleasures – do not appeal to all young people, by any means. Many seventeen- to twenty-year-olds hold fast to dreams of pure relationships of friendship and love. But often, lacking support, these feelings expire or are overwhelmed by cynicism. We felt obligated to help these teens get together, find each other, and strengthen their internal aspirations toward spirituality. By spending time together, they cease to feel different, like "white crows," and stop fighting with the better aspects of their souls. Kids at that age are desperately drawn to the company of adults, even though, having accumulated disappointments, they sometimes go to great lengths to hide that desire. Interaction with teens of this age group and instruction in religious education are very delicate undertakings and demand special preparation and great care.

From the very beginning I tried not to attract the teens to myself personally, so as not to block God or interfere with the formation of their personalities. At the same time my attempts to be fully tolerant during the first year were unsuccessful. I was convinced – and the kids, surprisingly, agreed with me – of the need for strict discipline, even though we limited strictness to a specific sphere of issues. Gradually, through trial and error, we came up with a specific rule for the community. Everyone should, if only for one year, attend classes in catechism. Everyone was obliged to perform some kind of work for the community as a whole, such as kitchen duty, cleanup of the church and the surrounding area, and church penances. No one, except the confessor and director of the community, had a right to claim any sort of privileged role in the group, to make judgments, to administer reprimands, and so on.

I will be so bold as to offer some recommendations for those who intend to lead spiritual conversations with young people and perhaps create a youth community.

- One must somewhat strictly see that parents and people over the age of thirty do not attend youth activities and studies. Their presence will impede unconstrained interaction. As our experience of failure showed, even the most democratic "older people" occasionally give in to a wish to "muzzle" a young person or to "put him in his place." The community should provide young people with a secure space for interaction.

- Good theoretical training is essential for the teacher or leader of the community and, most important, he or she must be able to lead discussions correctly and competently.

- Under no circumstances should one allow oneself to exert even the slightest pressure through recourse to one's own authority or the church's.

- Never gloss over difficult issues by resorting to vague language. It is better to admit one's incompetence and promise to research the question for the next time. Be sure to do so!

- In arguments, it is better to appeal first to reason and only secondarily to the heart, since young people often lack the essential experience in matters of the heart.

- Except among groups of juvenile criminals, we rarely speak of sin and repentance among youth audiences. The typical young person interprets such conversations as yet another boring reprimand (just as adult women interpret even a reprimand as a sign that they are not meaningless, which explains the success of "strict" priests).

- It is useless to scare youth by discussing what could happen to them after death, since at that age death seems like an abstraction.
- Particular emphasis must be placed on the following principles:

1. Man was created free, which means fully responsible for good and evil.

2. The uniqueness of each individual is precious to God, but the more pure one is, the more one is inimitable. (All worthless people are alike, but saints are inimitable.) And it is important to speak clearly about the saints – not using the embellished saints' lives, but rather using historical documents.

3. For the church as the Body of Christ, *your* personality is valued and unique. (St. Justin: "When you were outside the church, there was a wound in the body of the church, which no one except you could heal.")

4. It is essential to cultivate an "adoration" for all the talents given you by God.

5. Love of God, of parents, of people, marital love, inner spiritual and holy love.

- If ritual, ceremonial questions arise, one must substantiate them from as many different points of view as possible: rational, symbolic, aesthetic. Never simplify anything or show how everything in Orthodoxy is a beautiful and harmonious whole.
- After lessons it is good to have tea and together read and learn the evening rule, as often as possible asking the kids for help. But one must work with them oneself.
- Very helpful in bringing groups of young people together are joint excursions to holy places and multi-day camping trips.

Three times we went to Optina Abbey, in 1992, 1994, and 1996. Each time more and more kids participated in the trip, and the trips became increasingly well organized. The last time thirty people participated – almost the entire community at that time. From the pilgrimage we brought back to Kazan' parts of the bones of canonized Optina elders. Now the kids organize pilgrimages on their own to monasteries and sacred places in the Kazan' diocese – they lead groups of children and parents who are newcomers to Sunday school. Our long-standing and probably unrealizable dream is to have our own bus.

After I became a nun, in November 1994, I moved to a small church, the only one remaining at the site of the Monastery of Our Lady of Kazan'. Our church was formerly above the gate in the surrounding walls of the monastery. Now the passageway under the arched gate has become a refectory; as need arises it can be transformed into a classroom or a concert hall. On the walls, the massive hinges of the gates have been preserved to this day. We often say that probably we aren't yet up to the real monastery, so they left us at the entrance. And yet this is the entrance to a sacred place, the place where the Kazan' icon of the Mother of God is found. As is well known, a young girl found the icon, and as in olden times, Our Lady today is favorably disposed toward children and youth here.

Finally a refuge had emerged for the youth community, which now began to grow rapidly. We were given our own priest for the community, also quite young, with a special blessing given by the higher orders of clergy to his nourishing of young people. In time he took under his wing all the young men, and I basically worked with the young women. Of course, such a division of duties is extremely conventional. Working together with Father Sergei is a great joy for me. The kids and I often wonder how, out of all the priests in Kazan', we happened to get the best and most fascinating. And here's another interesting thing: in a community where a good half are very young girls, the young and likable priest manages to stand firm with such tact that in four years there has never been a single case of unhappy romantic attachment. Unfortunately, this situation happens fairly often in other parishes, even with parishioners who are not at all young.

Once again it was time to think about customs in the community, somehow to adjust the code of discipline. Everyone agreed with the dry law on the community premises: at that time we had quite a few school-age youth, and we could not permit someone to smell of alcohol after visiting the church. And it seemed important to me, moreover, that the kids understand and remember how happily and freely one can socialize without any help from alcohol. Along with Father Sergei, we paid special attention at first to the purity of the relationships among the youth of the community. We tried gently to put an end to the first indications of frivolous, free-and-easy behavior. We said that our place was special, that it was under the protection of the Mother of God. We could not sully this place by our vulgar behavior and turn it back into a place like all the others around us. Then we would have no place to seek shelter. This worked like silk, and soon the need for such conversations disappeared. The new kids automatically emulated the kind of behavior accepted in the community.

A majority of the kids came to us from nonbeliever families, some from Muslim families (roughly half the members of our group are Tatars). We didn't manage to avoid all family conflict, but the kids behaved mildly and tactfully; they invited their parents to visit the community and received them with honor. Soon many of the mothers joined the ranks of our parishioners. There were far fewer problems with our current crop of new members. The relationship of the laymen to the church has become more tolerant.

Three to four girls live with me in the church constantly. They are not future nuns. It is simply that first one, then another of the girls of the community are so enthusiastic about our common life and work that, with the agreement of their parents, they move in with us for a long stay. For the past two years a twelve-year-old girl has been brought up in our community. Before that, she had grown up in such a terrible family situation that even in winter, fearing to return home, she would stand on the street until far into the night. We would be happy to take in several more such half-homeless children, but for the time being we have no room to do so. We do not make it our mission to educate future nuns and monks. We merely try to free the girls from the obsession that it is shameful to remain unmarried. It is very important that every person understand himself and find his true calling.

It is interesting that three or four years ago the kids would come with categorical statements: "We aren't going to study; we don't need secular studies; we're only going to work in the church." With time they all settled down and entered institutes; two or three even started graduate school. Now we have various specialties: programmer, veterinarian, dentist, psychologist, sociologist, economist, designer, meteorologist. Eight boys entered the Kazan' theological college, and three have become priests. In four years only one girl and one boy have entered monastic life, and right now no one else is expressing intentions of that kind.

Our church is renowned for its beautiful girls' choir. Its story is rather unusual. Eight years ago, when I had just begun to work in the cathedral, an amateur girls' choir was formed. Among the girls one stood out, a very young girl of seventeen, but with outstanding leadership and vocal qualities. Together with a girlfriend, also a student at the school of music, she occasionally sang at the cathedral, but the two were in great disfavor. They were considered frivolous, and actually they were frequently late and would also miss services. But there was no way to dismiss them, because they had agreed to sing without payment. The girls' choir was of no use to anyone at all, however, because on weekdays the girls went to school, and on Sundays a choir of professional vocalists sang at the cathedral. At times the girls would go to sing at remote country churches, trying to get there by hitching rides from passing traffic, in freezing weather, and in periods when the roads were flooded.

When we were given the Church of St. Sophia, I asked that these girls be transferred to me, although I had tried my best to turn down professional female vocalists. The authorities thought I was crazy, but they agreed, since choristers at that time were in short supply. I couldn't have made a better choice. After heading the church choir and becoming more adult, the girls naturally stopped being late. Little by little they recruited five more persons, and now we have an unusually united group in our chancel. Incidentally, as far as I know this is the only choir in Kazan' in which all the singers are believers. And one indication of their professionalism is the fact that three members of our choir took part in a church choir competition in Rome last year, and this group placed second, just behind the sponsors of the competition. Now two of the choristers are studying at the conservatory, and the others are at the academy of fine arts, training to become choir conductors.

Last year yet another job was found for the choristers. Unofficially at first, we organized a children's school of liturgical singing. We had made similar attempts since 1989 and had engaged highly qualified precentors, but we couldn't get things off the ground: the children sang abominably. And every year they would explain to me that it was an impossible undertaking. Finally our girl choristers took over, and the choir became a success. This spring our *Vladyka* officiated at a special children's liturgy in the church, and he was stunned to hear how marvelous the children's voices sounded. It seemed to me at the time that some kind of trickery was involved for here were such small children with such a powerful sound. Since September we have conducted official recruitment for the choral school, which will turn out professional church singers in four years. The students are learning to read music and do solfeggio, and they are also taught the history of liturgical singing. And our girls do all the work for token wages of $7.50 per month, the usual salary of our teachers. We are promised that restoration of a special children's church will be finished quite soon. It will be located not far from the school, and in it there will be a special refectory for the children. We hope that the parents of the little singers will become permanent members of the church parish.

The Church of St. Sophia has become not only a shelter, but also an object of the youth's concern. Work in the church teaches the kids that they themselves *are* the church. Unfortunately, even among adult parishioners a narrowly practical attitude toward the church is now characteristic, a notion that "everyone everywhere owes them something." Our kids themselves participate in the worship service as psalm readers and subdeacons. The telephone at the Church of St. Sophia is well known to parishioners throughout the entire city: the boys and girls of the community always respond to believers' requests to read the Psalter at the bedside of a deceased relative or to sing the office for the dead at funerals. In the winter of 1996–1997, the youth independently did a major overhaul of all the church buildings. The boys, under the priest's direction, did the essential carpentry and construction work: they rebuilt the sanctuary – the part of the chancel containing the high altar – and made shelves for the school library, stands, and collecting boxes for offerings.

Because of the extremely limited means allotted for school maintenance, the kids were forced to collect offerings on the city streets. We were especially in need of funds in 1997, when our cherished dream was fulfilled: we were given a beautiful building for the school. But we had to furnish it and put it into shape ourselves. Over the course of the year we succeeded not only in furnishing the school's classrooms attractively and sensibly, but also in finding benefactors who donated a computer and an old Xerox machine to us. They assigned us a separate room for the library – and we were able to organize a city-wide Orthodox library with a ticket system and a reading room. After a year, more than one thousand volumes were assembled there. Our pupils work four times a week as librarians, without payment. In fall 1997, the work of the school and the community was raised to a new qualitative level.

Besides the Church of St. Sophia, a fundamental focus of our youth's energies is missionary work and teaching at the school. From this point of view, the youth are the most promising, vitally important group of the population. Depending on their aptitude, some of our kids chose work with children, while others decided to work with adults. At the present time, nine young teachers are working at the school. Branches of the school have appeared in remote areas of the city, since we now have a sufficient number of trained teachers to supply any demands. We often are invited to give presentations in hospitals and military units, before members of the police force and at places of imprisonment, and in schools, colleges, and universities.

In addition to missionary talks and lectures, the kids can present a concert of sacred songs or put on a little show. For three years now the community has had a youth theater. Twice a year the members of the community organize Christmas and Easter matinées for the Sunday school pupils. The kids have composed and produced for the children such plays as "About the Little Girl Matrona" (a play dedicated to the finding of the Kazan' icon of the Mother of God), "Little Sister Alenushka, Little Brother Ivanushka, and the Persian Merchant Artoban," "The Coming of the Antichrist and the Pious Lad," and "Palm Sunday." Sometimes, someone's birthday or name-day is celebrated on the community premises, and then the tea drinking has to be accompanied by an impromptu concert. At some such young people's parties, *Vladyka* Anastasii himself is present. Now the theater is experiencing its second youth: a group of young people who joined us this fall are bent on entertaining us with puppet shows.

An important event in the life of the community was the creation in the school of a children's scout troop in spring 1998. From its earliest days the troop has grown quickly to thirty members, and it continues to grow. The scouting movement has made it possible to attract children between twelve and fourteen to Sunday school and keep them there. Previously this age group was virtually lost to us. The children who for several years had attended lessons with their parents lost all interest in them about the time they turned twelve, and they even stopped going to church services.

At the age of sixteen or seventeen they sometimes returned, but some left the church permanently. Now teens between twelve and fourteen are our mainstay and a source of support in our work with younger kids. We accept members into the troop from the age of eight or nine on, and the older ones learn to take the young kids under their wing. This is done especially touchingly during out-of-town camping trips. In summer, on the banks of the Volga, we had a big two-week camp called "The First Christians." In the fall there was a three-day camp session in town, during which all the scouts spent the night and ate at the Church of St. Sophia. During the winter vacation, before Christmas, we intend to take the children to the picturesque hamlet of Pitiial.

Another important means of educating the scout troop was the extraordinary revelation of hitherto undisplayed abilities of our youth. Among the members of the community, almost everyone was in one way or another occupied in working at the school. Scouting called forth an explosion of creative activity in our kids and stimulated the rapid growth of their leadership and administrative qualities. The troop leader, a twenty-two-year-old young woman, and her helpers and youth leaders work practically without needing any help from adults. Several times a week the scouts visit a shelter for orphaned children, and there, playing and spending time with the young kids, they demonstrate what the scout lessons have taught them. The scouts also are helping in the renovation of the buildings of the ancient Zilantov Monastery. Since fall 1998, the school program has been supplemented by a group known as "Skillful Hands," in which the children learn to make not only toys, but also articles for church use. We hope that the sale of these articles at the Easter fair will fatten the school's purse somewhat.

To improve the qualifications of our young teachers and to help middle-school teachers who want to introduce instruction in the origins of Christianity into their curriculums, missionary courses began in our Sunday school in September 1998. Our youth do more than merely attend such courses. A twenty-five-year-old teacher with seven years of experience as a Sunday school teacher gives the lectures on the Gospels, and lectures on adult psychology are presented by students in the psychology and sociology departments at Kazan' State University.

Over the past year, as happens in youth groups, we had an "epidemic" of weddings. Of four couples, three were formed within the community. In February 1999, we expect the birth of the first two representatives of the second generation. We have already started to consider that it might be time to stop accepting people into the community because of lack of space. In our refectory, with the best will in the world there is room for no more than fifty persons. At our festive table, especially at Easter, there are more and more "standing" places. But we won't succeed in discontinuing admission. This fall fifteen more persons came to the lessons of the youth group, and the majority of them do not intend to restrict themselves to catechism lessons, but want to join the community. The swift growth of the community causes some anxiety, in light of the immutable capacity of the buildings; however, we can't deny newcomers who conscientiously wish to work for the church and their fellow men their right to be alongside us.

On Christian Psychology

The study of psychology is our new interest and new program for work with youth. Thus it happened that over the past years several people with educations in psychology came to us. It is necessary to point out that we were already interested in psychology previously; necessity had led us to that pursuit.

In the early years of the community's existence, kids with family and church problems would often come to us. With regret we noticed that the church problems were created by inept, but extremely rigid spiritual leadership. Every spiritual mentor basically proceeds from his own experience, from the needs of his own psychological type. The fact that all people are different is unknown to many inexperienced priests, and for some this notion is altogether unacceptable. That means that neuroses among the congregation are inevitable in those cases where spiritual leaders try to make an extrovert into an introvert, and vice versa. Some kids, who had persistently been pushed to cut short their educations and enter a monastery or a convent, were in despair, on the verge of a breakdown. One boy, who in childhood had suffered from a severe stammer, after going to church practically lost his ability to speak once more; he started to suffer from insomnia and severe headaches. Meanwhile, these kids were highly intelligent and were trying to understand what was going on with them.

We started to investigate things together. In 1995 and 1996, we conducted a cycle of talks and seminars on a great variety of topics: the Christian relationship to art, laughter, and humor; emotional and spiritual love. We conducted several pedagogical, psychological, and psychiatric seminars with the participation of experts. Our *Vladyka* gave us a great deal of support in this work. We drew out the kids, and a more or less reasonable relationship to many acute problems was established.

I had to study psychology more deeply, and the knowledge I acquired helped me solve several personal problems, which, however strange it may be, had not been solved through confession. And I came to understand that one successfully complements the other. Thus the idea arose, and with time became stronger, to create in the church a committee for psychological consultation. A consulting psychologist could examine with a parishioner his urgent problems, which in turn would be an excellent preparation for the sacrament of confession.

In 1998, a theological college was opened in Kazan'. There arose a notion to introduce into the program a short course in Christian psychology, but nothing worthwhile came to light in the literature. There were only artificial conglomerations of quotes from the Fathers of the church and snippets of general psychology, without any ties to actual practice. At the present time a small group of our young psychologists are preparing a course in Christian psychology for the seminary, and at the same time they are preparing to create a committee for psychological counseling. Of course, such a bold undertaking will eventually require a financial outlay, but we hope that if this idea is in accordance with God's will, then the means will be found.

The Significance of the Orthodox Youth Movement

It is difficult to say whether in our times people have begun to suffer with particular acuteness from spiritual discomfort, or whether in a century of mass information, spiritual problems too have begun to be discussed more loudly. In any event, these problems exist and call attention to themselves. It is interesting that people in East and West are suffering from diametrically opposed things. In the industrialized Western countries people suffer from isolation and, as a result, from loneliness. In the African and Asian countries people are smothered by close dependence on the social context. People in our country, not yet recovered from the suffocating grip of a totalitarian regime, are rapidly gravitating toward Western individualism. We have started to forget that there exists another type of relationship between people: Christian relationship; love through the Lord, when, loving God, we love all those who are dear to Him. Yet everyone who loves and is loved retains both his freedom and his originality. The people in the early Christian communities related to one another in this way. We also need to learn how to relate to each other in this way, since the times in which we now live more than anything else recall the apostolic times. No one comes to the church unthinkingly and because of tradition. Each person's path to God is unique and distinctive; each person is called in his own particular way.

The position of youth in Russia is unique right now. Their parents' generation is in disarray. All the previous values have collapsed. Everything their own parents had urged upon them – getting an education, living quietly and resignedly pending receipt of a pension – has no kind of value now. The schools, accustomed to looking to directives from above, also withdrew from education. The youth were left to their own resources, and, naturally, they are trying to survive in new conditions. The conditions of life increasingly recall the "Wild West," so information for survival is being drawn from westerns. The consequences are obvious.

But just now, when everything in Russia is rocking on its foundations and collapsing, the church is growing and gaining strength. Apparently the church is destined to gather around it all the viable forces of society. I often have to give talks among the most "depraved," "incorrigible" teenagers, in vocational and technical schools that pride themselves on their gangs of thugs and in colonies for juvenile criminals. Each time, after my talk, there are dozens of questions about confession and about opportunities to turn over a new leaf. Of course, conversations are not enough; systematic work is needed. And it must be done in the first place with children, before they have begun to be drawn to evil. And there are still so few of us! There is so little we are able to do!

Divine Providence leads kids with pedagogical abilities, psychologists, and sociologists to our community. All this, of course, is not accidental; the Lord reveals our mission in this world. In the community the youth find friendship, friendship united with concerted work. This is not acquaintanceship for dances and flirting, but friendship for life. It is impossible to set fire to the soul of another person if your own soul has grown cool. It is impossible to teach others pure, decent relationships if you yourself have lost the art of being friends.

The misfortune of contemporary Christians is their estrangement. Even the most earnest parishioners come to church as if to a movie theater, and, after standing through the service, they part and go their separate ways. And Christianity is left behind at the church. The study of Christian love is based on experience. Life in a community, constant work side by side: these things teach tolerance and sympathy. Conflicts and clashes occur, but all of us are Christians, all of us are trying to become better, and all of us have our own difficulties. Today you forgave someone; tomorrow you will be forgiven. You won't learn that lesson in theory. It seems to me that only communal life is Christian life.

There should be more communities such as ours, as many as possible, throughout Russia. And the main thing is that the kids in the communities should be educated not as obedient dischargers of duties, but as leaders, as creators. Otherwise, nothing will be gained. Can this be somehow planned or organized? No, of course not, just as it is impossible to plan a living tree. We can only do all that we are able toward such an end – and pray. What man cannot do, God can.

Plans and Problems

1. *Organization of an annual all-Russian camp for young church workers.* It is possible that we are not alone. Unfortunately, I know

nothing about other youth communities, but that does not mean that there aren't any. As a rule, we turn to Moscow for information, but in Moscow, as it turns out, the situation in the Orthodox Church is most unfavorable. Everyone has broken up into little groups, fighting among themselves for incomprehensible and insignificant reasons. The people who do not want to participate in such an absurd struggle are demoralized and dispersed.

For that reason, I think that a most important task is to begin to gather the working, healthy multitude of Orthodox youth, focusing mostly on the provincial cities. For several years I have been planning a two-week camp outing on the banks of the Volga, a seminar for young church workers. Work should be conducted in separate groupings: for young priests, for Psalm readers, for precentors, for teachers, and for scout leaders. If our plans interest Orthodox youth in America and other countries, the camp could be international, which would extend the perspective of the participants and render petty divisions insignificant.

2. *The necessity of having our own means of transportation.* This is a problem, rather than a plan, because for the time being we see no hope of equipping ourselves with transportation. Meanwhile, our work is suffering great damage. A majority of the pupils at our school are children from very poor families, and some can be considered practically orphans. For such children, travel by public transportation to the camp, and at times also from home to Sunday school, is an expenditure beyond their means. It is very annoying when a long-awaited and important measure fails because of the lack of transportation. For example, this year our kids were invited to Zelenodol'sk to meet with local youth. A real chance appeared to broaden our work and create a youth community in a neighboring town, but the meeting failed to take place because of transportation difficulties. The availability of even one bus of our own would allow us to make regular pilgrimage excursions to holy places, meet with youth from neighboring towns, and go on concert and missionary tours. It would solve the problem of getting the scout troops to the campsite and bringing the children from the shelter to Sunday

school. But for the time being we can only pray and put our trust in the Lord.

3. *Transition to the creation of a community encompassing all age groups.* I am sure that it is possible to create Christian communities for all age groups and generations, not just youth, which would give rise to a truly Orthodox family. For this reason I am asking that our work be regarded as one of the first and not-yet-complete attempts to create something of this type. Consider it a "laboratory" version, a primitive version. Evidently I, as the leader of this Christian community, four years ago simply lacked the strength to gather around myself people who were older than I in age and spiritual experience. Recently, as part of our scout camp we were able to bring together sixty people of various generations and social strata for a two-week joint excursion, and the experience was very successful. This problem is somewhat new to me; in solving it I am sure that we will encounter quite unexpected difficulties. It is possible that to join together various age groups into one community, one must already have conducted separate development among parishioners of each age group. Given that I already have experience working with a group of scouts' parents (mothers and grandmothers), I do not see any major difficulties in this. I dream of learning about the experience of Catholic communities of this type, which exist, as I now understand, in America.

4. *The creation as soon as possible within the church of a committee for psychological counseling.* At present we are working with great seriousness on the realization of this aim. We are trying to look at the contemporary achievements of practical psychology with the eyes of the ancient ascetics and church Fathers. This helps us to interpret correctly many features of church practice and adapt psychological techniques to the consciousness of Orthodox parishioners.

Besides a lack of material resources, in our work we also lack experienced consultants and counselors. As is well known, psychological studies were in a wretched state during the years of Soviet power. I know that the United States is a huge center of contemporary psychological studies. I very much hope to meet in America with experienced practical and social psychologists and with specialists in the psychology of spiritual life. If the program of our work interests foreign colleagues, we could develop a joint program. But in any case, I hope that two years from now the first clients will be receiving psychological consultation consistent with the views and moral standards of the Orthodox Church, and that students at the Kazan' seminary will begin to study the origins of Christian psychology.

Conclusion

Of course, I have not given an exhaustive account of everything that has been done and experienced by our community or everything that we plan to do in the future, especially since, in a group like ours, life moves at a rapid pace and new plans are born each day. But I have tried hard to create in American readers of this chapter as true as possible an impression of our work; an impression of the creation of our community not as the assembling of a structure according to blueprints, but as the careful, tremulous nurturing of a marvelous plant sown by Our Lord Himself.

I am very grateful to you all for your interest in our work and our life. And if my story perhaps can help you solve some problems of your own that are unknown to me, I will consider that my task has been accomplished.

BUILDING AN ETHICAL CIVIL

SOCIETY THROUGH JUSTICE

IRINA V. RESHETNIKOVA

Irina V. Reshetnikova, Ph.D., is a professor of law in the Department of Civil Procedure at the Ural State Law Academy in Ekaterinburg. An extraordinarily productive writer, she has been published extensively in the area of law and in the field of textbooks. She has served as a visiting professor at University College, London, and was a Fulbright Scholar at the University of Michigan Law School. Now involved in the important tasks of developing a new legal culture and training future generations of lawyers, here Professor Reshetnikova outlines ways to undergird civil society and the rule of law in Russia.

BEFORE WE SPECULATE about ways to build an ethical civil society in Russia, we need to answer this question: What constitutes an ethical civil society? There are various approaches to the issue, of course, because such a society has moral, religious, legal, and a host of other components. Those parts of the larger whole have certain features in common, however, and I will focus on them because they reveal what already has been done to build an ethical society in Russia, what problems still remain, and how those problems can be solved.

The first sign of a civil society is that the state recognizes human rights and freedoms. Before enumerating specific rights, the state has to decide whose interests and rights are of paramount importance. Soviet law, for example, sought to protect the state and the property of the state above all else. Human rights were at the foot of the list. In 1993 a very important legislative step was taken: Article 2 of the Constitution of the Russian Federation declared that "Man and his rights and freedoms are the highest value. Recognition of, compliance with, and defense of the rights and freedoms of man and the citizen shall be the duty of the state." However, we still apply Soviet-era legislation, such as the Code of Civil Procedure and the Code of Criminal Procedure, which date from the 1960s. According to the law, then, the courts still are obliged to protect the interest of the state first. Obviously Russia needs to introduce new, modern legislation as quickly as possible.

Having recognized human rights and freedoms as the highest value, the state has to enumerate basic rights and freedoms: All men are born free and equal; basic rights are inalienable and belong to every human being from birth. The Russian Constitution has proclaimed many fundamental rights and freedoms, including the right to life, the right to freedom, and the right of personal inviolability. Further proof of the state's acknowledgment of inalienable rights was given in 1996, when the Russian Federation joined the Council of Europe. However, no one is under the illusion that the mere proclamation of rights and liberties is sufficient evidence that a civil society is likely to appear soon. Proclamation of rights must be followed by a second, crucial step: protection of those rights.

The second sign of a civil society is that the state properly protects human rights and freedoms. In this area, we in modern Russia face many problems. According to the Constitution, everyone is guaranteed the right to receive qualified legal assistance, for example. But can Russians get access to that assistance if teachers, doctors, workers, and others receive no salary for months on end and thus cannot afford to hire any kind of advocate? In only a few cases is free assistance available; most people have to pay for legal services. Economic or legal obstacles prevent the exercise of other rights and freedoms as well. Protection of human rights and freedoms is not yet satisfactory.

The third sign of a civil society is that the government tries to create conditions for a decent standard of living. As long as its people have many rights but live in poverty, we cannot describe a society as "civil." The statistics tell a powerful story: In 1998, the minimum monthly wage in Russia was $3.90, yet $35.80 and below per month is recognized as a poverty-level income. The average monthly wage was $88.60. A mere 1.5 percent of the Russian population own 65 percent of all Russia's wealth. Comments are superfluous; the figures speak eloquently for themselves. And of the 250-odd factors that influence the level of crime in the Russian Federation today, the poor economy is the most important.

The fourth sign of a civil society is that the state recognizes the judiciary as the third branch of power, equal in authority to the legislative and executive branches. This recognition has been granted in Russia.

The fifth sign of a civil society is that obedience to the law and respect for the rights of other people are standard conduct. It is not only the state that has to contribute toward the building of a civil society; every citizen has to lay a brick in its foundation. Unfortunately, in Russia there exists a strong tradition of "legal nihilism," extreme skepticism regarding the law and the judicial system. There are many reasons for the rejection of belief in justice.

The sixth sign of a civil society is that the law is based on such principles as democracy and humanism. In this sense, law can help strengthen the ethics of society. The precept that "parents must take care of their children" is one such ethical principle. Russian legislation reflects the same moral code, and if a parent breaks the legal rules, he or she may be punished, for example, by being required to make support payments or by being deprived of parental rights. Even criminal law contains protections for some ethical rules. The Bible warns "Thou shalt not kill," for example. And criminal legislation provides punishment for the commission of murder. In criminal and civil litigation, all privileges reflect and protect society's ethical values, including communication between parent and child, priest and parishioner, doctor and patient, and husband and wife. Law that is based on ethical principles is inherently more democratic and conforms more closely to the requirements of a civil society. Moreover, such a society also needs political pluralism, democratic institutions, a policy of *glasnost'*, or public openness, and market relations.

Let us imagine a pair of scales. Into one scale pan we put all our rights and freedoms, into the other we place remedies for the protection of those rights and freedoms. Only if the pans balance is it possible to say "We have a civil society." For Russia, it is too soon to make that assertion. Three of the hallmarks of a civil society listed above are real problems in Russia: lack of real defense of certain rights and freedoms; "legal nihilism"; and a poor standard of living. The third can be solved only through economic reform. The other two, however, can be overcome through the use of legal remedies, including judicial proceedings.

Now I would like to suggest *how we can move toward an ethical civil society through justice,* how we in Russia can solve some of the problems troubling us today. According to the Russian Constitution, "To each shall be guaranteed the judicial defense of his rights and freedoms" (Article 46, Part 1). How can we create remedies to protect those entitlements? Let us take civil litigation as an example. The main tendency of modern civil litigation in Russia is the development of *adversarial trial.* Historically, Russian litigation, like that of the rest of the Continent, was based on an inquisitorial system. In an inquisitorial trial the judge plays a very active role, by collecting evidence, reviewing case materials, questioning witnesses, reaching a decision, and the like. The parties are passive and often participate in the trial without advocates.[1]

Russian civil justice is no longer completely inquisitorial, of course; since 1864 our litigation has been based on certain principles of the adversarial process, including oral and open trial and participation by persons representing the parties. Civil litigation in our country, then, does not follow the classic model of the inquisi-

---

1. In Russia there may be additional historical reasons for the activeness of the judge's role. The 1917 Revolution was followed by a period of conflict between the old and new regimes. Many Russian lawyers did not want to support the Soviet government, which abolished pre-1917 institutions: the law, the courts, the bar, and the prosecutor's office. At that time many of the new judges had no legal education, and educated advocates were reluctant to represent parties in a trial. New legislation was still being developed, and sometimes judges had to have recourse to prerevolutionary legislation. Moreover, this was a period of decisive class struggle for power in the new state. The court reflected the authoritarian regime and played an active role in settling all disputes.

torial system, but it is not yet truly adversarial.[2] Two prominent inquisitorial characteristics are still typical of Russian justice: (1) The law plays a more important role than court practice (the so-called principle of the supremacy of statutory law); (2) The judge plays a very active role in a trial. Historically, Russian law was based on Roman law, and that relationship explains our lack of case law. Court practice depends on the law, and all legislation concerning criminal and civil justice can be adopted only by the Parliament of the Russian Federation. The role of court practice has increased, however.[3]

For many years Russian judges had to exercise functions that in other countries are shared by the lawyers of the parties, judges, clerks, and masters. Until 1995, the courts were obliged not to be limited by the evidence submitted and to make every effort to obtain all possible evidence in the case. Now, however, the situation is different. The Constitution admits the adversarial approach as a principle of justice. In accordance with the Constitution, the Code of Civil Procedure introduced new rules in 1995.[4] Now the parties, not the judge, collect evidence and present it to the court in accordance with the burden of proof. A judge may order expert testi-

2. In the United States and the United Kingdom the general opinion is that Russian civil litigation belongs to the inquisitorial system. Some Polish scholars now suggest that all Continental procedures belong to the mixed form and include characteristics of both inquisitorial and adversarial systems.

3. Case law can play a variety of roles. For example, the court can introduce rules that are not present in the legislation, and it can interpret and even change rules. In Russia, the Plenum of the Supreme Court and the Plenum of the Highest Arbitration Court are entitled to interpret legal rules, and the resolutions of those plenums are binding on all courts. Still, this is not case law. According to Russian legislation, the courts have no right to adopt any law. Some decisions of the Supreme Court and the Highest Arbitration Court play the role of case law; other courts hearing similar cases must take their decisions into account.

4. The introduction of new rules did not solve every problem. For example, Russian civil procedure does not bind the parties to exchange the pleadings and evidence in the case. Therefore, before the case is heard the parties have no idea what will be under discussion at the trial.

mony, and he may help the parties obtain evidence if the party is able to name the evidence, explain why he could not obtain it himself, and state who possesses it.

A judge decides a case on the basis of the evidence produced for examination in trial. At the same time, under Article 50 of the Code of Civil Procedure, the court defines what circumstances are important to the case and which party is obliged to prove them. The court puts them up for discussion, even if the parties have not made reference to them. The court also has the right to ask the parties to produce additional evidence.[5]

To prove a case, then, the parties have to seek professional legal assistance; otherwise, they cannot make proper use of the machinery of justice.[6] They are not acquainted with procedure, nor do they usually know what they will hear during the trial. The parties alone cannot prepare a case for trial and examination of the evidence. At the present time, the parties have lost the assistance of the judge in the pretrial period, and they have not yet been enabled to obtain adequate support by advocates in his stead.

The adversarial principle has to be balanced by the provision of a real chance to obtain professional assistance. Otherwise the concept of equality before the law and the court may become a figment, and then there will be no justice. But how can Russians pay for legal assistance? It is impossible to make the country's citizens prosperous overnight. Therefore the law has a duty to help people par-

5. Article 65 and Article 70 of the Code of Civil Procedure established this rule: If a party possesses documentary and real evidence and fails to produce it upon the demand of the court, the court has the right to consider that as an acknowledgment of the information contained in the evidence.

6. Under Russian law the parties have many important rights: They are entitled to read case files, make extracts and copies of case files, challenge the judge, exhibit and examine evidence, put questions to other people, participate in the trial, make motions, make arguments and present pleadings, argue all questions concerning the case, raise objections, appeal court decisions, and exercise other procedural rights. The parties can either protect their rights themselves or seek the help of lawyers.

ticipate in court proceedings. There are a few ways out of this dilemma.

The Code of Civil Procedure, for example, can help by drawing lawyers into civil litigation. In accordance with a court decision, the losing party pays the expenses of the successful party for the assistance of a legal representative. The payments must be within reason and must take the specific circumstances into consideration.

The American experience with *public-interest law* can also be applied here. American justice, which has relied on the adversarial principle from the beginning, has a long history of dealing with the problems confronting Russia now. In the early twentieth century, for example, Americans set up public-interest law firms to represent the poor in court, free of charge. Seventy years later American lawyers define the spheres that must be covered by public-interest law: poverty, civil rights, public rights, charitable organizations, justice, and the interests of racial and ethnic minorities, mental patients, consumers, and environmentalists. In all those spheres people can obtain legal aid free of charge or at greatly reduced charges. All those spheres, then, enjoy the protection of society.

Does Russia need public-interest law? Clearly, the answer is yes. The following explains why:

1. In Russia we see a rapid process of stratification of the population according to income. Many people cannot afford legal services.

2. The democratization of society has penetrated into the realm of law. Some groups – teenagers and mental patients, for example – have obtained wider rights than previously. That fact in itself is encouraging. Sometimes, however, members of such groups are unable to protect their own rights properly, and they become involved in criminal activity or fall victim to violence. We need to provide those members of society with special care and protections.

3. The development of a market economy requires extra guarantees for small businesses, which cannot afford to oppose large companies in a court trial.

4. Russian law has introduced the concept of the class-action suit, which can also be regarded as a subset of public-interest law.

In Russia we already have available certain legal institutions that engage in something similar to public-interest law. The prosecutor's office, trade unions, some social organizations, and state bodies can apply to the court to obtain defense of citizens' rights without charge. Those institutions have demonstrated their value over a period of eighty years, but they are not adequate to today's needs. We can promote the development of public-interest law in Russia in these ways:

1. New legislation on the legal profession should be adopted. We still apply the law of 1980.

2. Further support should be provided to the activities of the state bodies, state organizations, and prosecutors authorized to defend people in court.

3. The system of arbitration courts needs further development.

4. More legal services should be made available. Several years ago the number of lawyers in Russia was four times smaller than in France and fifteen times smaller than in the United States. That gap has narrowed somewhat. Further, we need to introduce special courses in trial advocacy for young attorneys. Many Russian law schools now include such courses in their curriculums.

5. We need to set up public-interest law firms and to institute tax privileges for lawyers who provide their professional services free of charge to those who cannot pay. One step in that direction is the founding of numerous legal clinics in Russia. Many have been organized under the auspices of law schools, and there students, under the supervision of professors and practicing attorneys, provide advice on legal matters and represent people who are unable to pay.

Class actions are another means of helping large groups of the population. Many Americans may regard class-action suits with suspicion, but in Russia the situation is different. In our country, class actions mostly involve the interests of consumers. In the mid-1990s, for example, millions of people lost their money because of widespread fraud and the collapse of banks. After August 17, 1999, many thousands more suffered because of the financial crisis in

Russia. Russian legislation does not provide for class actions in such cases; each plaintiff has to bring suit separately, so the judges have huge caseloads. As a result, only those people who filed first will be able to recover money from the defendant. All the other plaintiffs' cases will be heard too late to do them any good. If we permitted class actions in more types of cases, more plaintiffs would receive compensation.

There is one means of redress in Russia that comes close to class action. Any citizen, along with prosecutors, social organizations, and state bodies, may make a claim in a court of law if he believes that a piece of legislation violates human rights or that the actions of state bodies, officials, or social organizations are wrongful. One citizen, for example, claimed that the charter of the region where he lives infringed on his rights and the rights of others to elect the governor of that region – and he won the case.

There may be other ways, too, to create an adversarial court within the reach of the average citizen. We could, for example, introduce summary proceedings in simple cases, introduce pleadings and discovery, and strengthen the *independence of judges*. According to the Constitution, of course, judges are independent and subject only to the Constitution and federal law. It is vital to safeguard that principle.

One of the most important guarantees of an independent judiciary is the public nature of the process of hearing cases in court. The openness of trial procedure distinguishes the activity of the courts from that of other bodies authorized to settle disputes. Trial procedure has some important features: legality; adherence to a detailed sequence of steps; clear definition of all stages of litigation; and obligatory observance of procedural rules by all parties concerned.

Other conditions, too, guarantee the independence of judges:

1. The requirements for becoming a judge are strict. For a long time, any Soviet citizen who was at least twenty-five years old could be elected to the bench. In 1989, 31.7 percent of the elected judges had no court experience. Some 250 of them had graduated from

law school within the past two years, and 417 had no higher legal education. Today possession of a law degree from an institution of higher learning is compulsory for judges. Additional requirements include at least five years of legal experience and the passing of a qualifying exam.

2. Judges are irremovable and inviolable.

3. Special procedures must be followed in order to terminate the employment of a judge.

Social and economic guarantees are important, too. The law confers many privileges upon judges in Russian society. When the state is short of funds, however, some of those privileges become inoperative.

There is one final problem: the *administration of justice*. Justice can be administered only when everyone is equal in a court of law. When people in Russia begin to believe that examination and determination of an issue between parties by a judge are helpful, they will start to believe in justice. And why do they not believe in it now? Here are some of the reasons:

1. The principal cause of public skepticism is poor enforcement of court decisions.[7] Even if someone wins a case, he will not necessarily receive compensation. Enforcement of civil court decisions is difficult. Last year, however, two new laws were adopted, and they may result in some progress in the area of enforcement procedure.

2. Plaintiffs have a long wait before their cases are scheduled for hearing, and people are reluctant to wait for justice to be done. Our law specifies how many days a case can be in the pretrial stage and

---

7. In addition to civil court decisions, other decisions must be enforced as well, including those rendered by commercial courts, bodies of arbitration, commissions, administrative bodies, and foreign courts. Moreover, execution officials work only at the district court level. In 1994, district courts received 6,197,000 execution documents, of which 23.9 percent originated with commercial courts, banks, and notaries. Each month an execution official works with about sixty documents and oversees five hundred or more documents.

when the hearing must begin.[8] Very often, however, courts cannot adhere to the rules because of the huge number of cases. In one district court, a judge had thirty-nine cases to try each month. Seven were criminal cases, fifteen, civil, and seventeen, administrative. In addition, like all other judges, he conducted pretrial hearings and supervised enforcement procedures.

3. Some people prefer to wait and let the judge collect the evidence for them, but times have changed. These days the losing party is very angry with a judge who failed to substantiate his burden of proof.

How are we to encourage a belief in justice, then? These suggestions may help:

1. Coordinate the activities of the bailiffs and the marshals of the courts, who can help in locating debtors and their property. This step also will support enforcement of court decisions.

2. The state can grant more economic support to the courts. All federal courts are financed by the state budget, but the funds they receive are inadequate. According to a selective poll, about 50 percent of Russia's judges say that the poor condition of the court buildings is a problem. Some district courts do not even have enough courtrooms. The courts cannot afford to have subpoenas served. Lack of adequate infrastructure can even contribute to infringements of the law, as this example shows: Often, civil cases have to be heard in the judge's consulting room, rather than a courtroom. Under the law, witnesses who have not yet testified have to be kept physically separate from witnesses who have given their testimony. In our district court, however, the buildings are tiny and all the witnesses have to wait their turns together in the corridor. Another ex-

8. Russian civil procedure includes these stages: pretrial; trial; cassation; reopening of a case in the exercise of supervisory power; reopening of a case upon discovery of new facts; execution. The pretrial stage may have two parts: institution of proceedings and preparation of a case for trial. First a judge has to determine whether proceedings may be instituted. Then the judge has several days – usually no more than twenty – to prepare the case for trial. In the pretrial stage the judge can call the parties for interview, order expertise, help the parties to collect evidence, and the like.

ample: The parties have a right to make a copy of the case documents, but there are no copying machines in the courts, so they must either write out the documents by hand or forego their right to a copy. Many parties choose to do the latter.

3. We can produce legislation based on democratic principles and rules.

In summary, then, legal remedies must be combined with economic remedies if we are to succeed in building an ethical civil society. The path toward that goal seems difficult and thorny, particularly in this time of economic and financial crisis in Russia, but if the state and the members of society can create the preconditions for justice, they will simultaneously move toward achieving that larger end.

THE BUILDING OF A CIVIL
SOCIETY AND THE MEDIA

LARISA MALINOVA

Larisa Malinova is director of the Management Center for the Electronic Media in Krasnoiarsk. The center, which is training a new generation of producers and managers for Russia's evolving independent television sector, teaches theoretical knowledge and arranges internships. Involved in direct management of a major television initiative serving central Siberia, Ms. Malinova is also the manager of a television station in Krasnoiarsk.

Changes in the Political Map: The Role
of the Media in the New Russia

IN THE PAST DECADE the political geography of the countries of Eastern Europe has changed utterly. This process was so swift that experts, both in those countries and abroad, were astonished. Moreover, a new influence on the political processes occurring in society has become evident: the electronic media of mass communication, in particular, television.

According to statistics from the Independent Sociological Agency, cited in "Television in Election Campaigns," 83.9 percent of Russia's inhabitants acquire various information from television broadcasts, 50.2 percent from newspapers, 43.3 percent from radio, and only 22.6 percent from direct contact with friends and relatives. Information that comes from the media undoubtedly is reinterpreted critically by many people. According to statistics from the same agency, slightly more than 20 percent of the population completely trust the information received from television. Nevertheless, television is undeniably a major influence on the value systems, social relations and attitudes, and behavior of many inhabitants of this country as it creates new democratic institutions.

The important role and enormous influence of the media are growing significantly in these difficult times for Russian society. That is especially true now, when the population has a choice to make; referendums and election campaigns are under way. Under these circumstances the media not only inform the population but also directly influence voters' preferences in a variety of ways: through the information policy pursued by media representatives, their methods of presenting information, the type of information presented, and outspoken assessments of the candidates' activities and personalities.

A special task of the mass media is to convince people to go to the polls. The most dangerous trend today is the disinclination of the most active segment of our nation – the people who are now creating a new society – to take part in elections. For if they don't vote, others will: "pensioners with a phenomenal memory that discards everything associated with the previous regime and retains only one thought: the feeling that life has gone by the rules, and it doesn't matter what kind of rules they were." [1] Or still others: people who, seeking a national concept around which to rally a society with severely damaged ties, will generate the notion of a "strong arm" or nationalism. Therefore, our chief task is to see that elections are held and to ensure participation in them by those citizens who are determining the economic, cultural, and social development of our society. That task is especially urgent in this year of elections to the State Duma, when, in the well-known words of the leader of the "Apple" faction in the Duma, Grigorii Iavlinskii, voters will determine not only the composition of the higher legislative body for the next four years, but the fate of the country for the next ten to fifteen years.

Do the media themselves realize their responsibility for the future of Russia and its democratic institutions? Aren't members of the media deceived when they emphasize their role and importance, calling themselves the "fourth power"? Whose interests

---

1. Interview with V. Vil'chek, the director of NTV Holding Company, a sociological analysis service, in 1998.

should this "fourth power" defend? What is the price of the media's independence?

A Short Analysis of Russia's Present-day Television Market

After the fall of the Soviet Union in 1991, the television industry experienced significant changes. Eight years ago virtually all television in Russia still belonged to the federal and regional authorities and operated under their direction and control. All the programs were produced by state companies or film studios. The financing of television came from the state budget; commercial advertising did not exist. Only two channels were genuinely national in scope. No market research on viewers' preferences was conducted.

Today in Russia, according to statistics from various sources, there are some six hundred television companies, including four hundred to five hundred non-state companies. The majority of the non-state companies have network agreements with one of the capital city's television channels (except ORT and VGTRK[2]). At least six non-state networks are trying to win a national audience, and all of them broadcast through the stations of their networks and transmit their programs via satellite.

A number of new, strong stations have appeared, and many of them have become leaders in their regions: Nizhnii Novgorod, Ekaterinburg, Tomsk, Krasnoiarsk, and Irkutsk. They offer their viewers alternative channels and programs that can compete with state news programs and that promote the development of openness in Russian society. The production of local television news made it possible for the first time to express the opinions and convey the interests of the local audience. That was an important event for the state, which has traditionally depended on centralized structures. Almost 50 percent of all Russians who watch television during prime time are viewers of non-state stations.

2. ORT = *Obshchestvennoe rossiiskoe televidenie*, Public Russian Television; VGTRK = *Vserossiiskaia gosudarstvennaia teleradio kompaniia*, All-Russian State Television and Radio Company.

Moreover, in the opinion of advertising experts, by fall 1997 there was already an obvious shift of emphasis from the central channels to the regional ones, and regional advertising markets independent of the center had appeared in Novosibirsk, Vladivostok, and southern Russia. In 1991, it was difficult even to imagine that the Russian television industry could develop in such a way. Commercial non-state television has found itself a stable niche in Russian culture and business.

Problems of Independent Television
in the Pre- and Post-crisis Periods

Although freedom of speech is considered the most positive change in Russia in the post-1985 period, the situation in the country's television market at the present time is far from realizing the hopes of the early years of *perestroika*. Today regional television in Russia is encountering numerous problems. Among the most important ones are these:

• the absence of a solid legal foundation and, as a consequence, the lack of any kinds of guarantees as we try to develop long-term business plans;

• the expansion of the Moscow media holding companies in the regional market, where they either conclude partnership agreements with stations or buy blocks of shares sufficient to veto or control major actions;

• dependence on local executive power: on the favor of the governors and heads of administrations; on the licensing policy pursued by regional communications workers and representatives of the Federal Television and Radio Service in the provinces; and

• the need for professional training of real value for the majority of workers at local stations.

Television, as an economic sector that depends on other sectors and subsists on advertising revenues, cannot develop faster than the other parts of the local economy. The crisis that began on August 17, 1998, struck every sphere of Russian life. The media were no exception. Experts estimate that the volume of advertising dropped by 50 to 70 percent. In September 1998, the economic indicators of the television company Afontovo plunged to the 1994 level. The station cut back on production of local programs, and new projects were put on hold. Some employees were placed on unpaid leave; others were laid off. Plans for providing the station with new technical equipment were postponed indefinitely.

Some fear that in these circumstances, on the eve of the presidential elections, there will be people who wish to pay the channels to promote one candidate or another. Movie distributors already are proposing that the regional television companies acquire films on a barter basis, in exchange for advertising time on the eve of the 2000 elections. Experts predict that in the current situation the local authorities will try to increase their influence on regional television, taking advantage of the fact that support from the federal government and Moscow financial groups has weakened.

The Development of a Civil Society and the Media

Let us look at the general characteristics of today's situation with regard to the media in the Krasnoiarsk region. Freedom of speech and access to information are prerequisites for the functioning of a democratic society. The realization of citizens' constitutional right to information depends to a significant extent on the activity of the media and on their ability to seek, receive, and disseminate information. Statistics from the Krasnoiarsk Fund for the Defense of Glasnost' indicate that among the sources of information about various spheres of life available to the inhabitants of the Krasnoiarsk region, the media rank first (up to 80 percent of information about politics). At the same time, from 36 to 60 percent of the inhabitants of the region's various territories are not satisfied with their level of informedness about various matters: events in their own region and in other parts of the country; how people live and what they think; situations at "hot points"; the activity of the federal and local authorities and deputies; the world of private enterprise and business; and the situation in neighboring regions.

These statistics, though not absolute, indicate that an "undocking" has occurred: there is a gap between the possibilities of the media and the needs of citizens for information. The statistics testify to the existence of problems in the system of mass communication.

A significant gap continues to exist between the "right to information" articulated over four years ago by Article 29 of the Constitution of the Russian Federation and the actual "receipt of information." The problem here lies not in the absence of the necessary legal foundation with regard to the media, but above all in the "legal nihilism" of the regime, society, and, unfortunately, journalists.

Not infrequently, former stereotypes of the relationship of the regime with the mass media still are active: the effort to control and subordinate the media to the will of those in power, and the attempt to punish dissidents in various ways, including the use of such powerful instruments as the court system. Officials and public politicians are not prepared for the heightened, constant, and frequently biased attention they receive from the media and public opinion. That is confirmed by the large number of conflicts in which the regional media and journalists have a hand. At the bottom of those conflicts lies a struggle for control of the channels of information.

In 1998, 130 conflicts with media participation were recorded in the Krasnoiarsk region. Analysis of the statistics shows that opposition to freedom of information occurs even before production and dissemination of the media's programs. That opposition first takes the form of "cutting off the oxygen" of the journalists by concealing the information they need (31.9 percent of all violations of the rights of the media and journalists) and interfering with professional journalistic activity (19.1 percent). Second, the significant number of "other violations" (38.3 percent) is evidence of a rich arsenal of means of exerting pressure on journalists. These examples suggest some of those means:

1. On August 17, 1998, A. I. Lebed', the governor of the region, signed a decree "On the Accreditation of Journalists from the Mass Media." The new regulations required that journalists carry accreditation passes for work in the administrative offices of the re-

gion. That requirement contradicts the Constitution and the law "On the Mass Media," which give all journalists the right to visit state bodies regardless of the availability or unavailability of accreditation.

2. In September letters were sent by the regional administration's Committee on Interaction with the Media to the editorial offices of the regional media, directing that "a written request be made three or four days in advance, in order to receive information or to arrange a meeting or an interview."

3. In April, unknown persons in camouflage uniforms severed antenna cables at the television company "Prima – TV." The cables supported the link with the satellite. In the opinion of journalists, it is not impossible that the incident was connected with the gubernatorial elections for the region.

4. In June, according to a report on the information channel "Top News," Governor Lebed' filed a suit in defense of his honor, dignity, and professional reputation against the Krasnoiarsk television and radio company Afontovo and against Dmitrii Rogozin, the leader of the Congress of Russian Communities, who had given an interview on the air to Afontovo, commenting on Lebed's methods of conducting his election campaign. The amount of the damages sought was 500,00 rubles from the station and 250,000 rubles from Rogozin: at the exchange rate of that time, before the August 1998 crisis, $74,000 and $37,000, respectively. One month later Lebed' withdrew his suit on the grounds that, in his opinion, the case was no longer of immediate interest. "Now that the election is over, we should not bear a grudge," he commented.

Incidentally, when Lebed' became the people's elected governor, Afontovo remained "afloat" only because of its timely joining of the "Media MOST" TV network. Otherwise, as A. Charkin, a correspondent of the newspaper *Izvestia*, notes, "the helpers of Aleksandr Ivanovich would have given no quarter to the oppositional 'mismanaged' television company. . . . Lebed' cannot interfere directly in the affairs of an independent television company. But for some reason, in the last few months guests from the FSB[3] and the tax inspector's office have taken to visiting Afontovo's offices." The employees at the government tax department had probably received specific assignments "to find something." However, no audit documents have been presented to Afontovo's management thus far.

The Krasnoiarsk state television and radio company "Center of Russia" apparently presented itself to Lebed' as the weakest link in the chain of "television saboteurs." Behind it there stands neither a Moscow media holding company nor a local oligarch. The conflict of Krasnoiarsk's Governor Lebed' with the management of the local region's state company recently evoked sharp criticism from not only the regional, but also the national independent media. The media noted the governor's dissatisfaction with the station's interpretation of events in the region and of his activities in particular, including his attempt to place a loyal henchman at the head of the company, although that action was a direct infringement of the legislation in force.

The governor has expressed, in his own original way, his dissatisfaction with the region's television as a whole. After four TV companies, invited by the governor's press service to a January conference on problems of the coal industry in the region, aired important stories with Lebed' using foul language, he suddenly announced during a meeting that the conference was a closed one, and that the television workers would pay for their actions by having their licenses revoked. The head of the Federal Television and Radio Service (FTRS), Mikhail Seslavinskii, who had written the governor a letter warning him against taking hasty action in regard to local television, reacted to the attack. The FTRS intends to investigate the situation of television in the Krasnoiarsk region in the immediate future.

Turning again to the statistics on conflicts involving the regional media in 1998, I must note that 37 percent of the cases involved vi-

---

3. FSB = *Federal'naia sluzhba bezopasnosti*, Federal Security Service.

olations of the rights of members of the media, but in 63 percent the violations were ascribed to editorial staff members and reporters. In 1997, those figures were 50 percent and 50 percent. What is behind these actions? The low level of journalism? The inability or unwillingness of journalists to check the facts? A poor command of vocabulary and language? Lack of education with regard to the law?

The main reason lies in the heightened desire of officials at all levels, politicians, and other "public persons," to take the press to task for having "overstepped the mark" and to show it its "proper place." It seems that proponents of censorship are mounting an offensive against freedom of speech and communication on all fronts. That assault is aided by the imperfection of the legislation; the inadequacy of judges' qualifications and, in some cases, their direct dependence on local authorities; and, unfortunately, the ignorance of the media themselves with regard to the law.

The principal group of violations that incriminate the media (49.4 percent) is made up of violations involving pre-election political agitation. This situation is completely understandable if we remember what fierce struggle elections have entailed in Russia in recent years and how involved all the media were in those battles. The 1998 gubernatorial election in Krasnoiarsk, where a fundamental struggle developed between "the region's own" acting governor V. Zubov and the "Varangian" A. Lebed', was an exception only to the extent of its bitterness. Not infrequently, it is quite difficult for journalists to investigate the complex conflicting processes taking place in society and the hidden mechanisms of the driving forces, as well as the goals, both declared and real, of influential social groups.

It is not easy to evaluate the true significance of the information that is received, to predict the development of events, and to determine the social consequences of various actions. In addition, during the period of the election campaigns, the candidates for high office also make use, in their political agitation and campaign publicity, of extremely intricate methods of influencing the voters' consciousness. The content and mechanisms of those methods are carefully concealed. In other words, the representatives of the media absolutely must have professional training and assistance in the interpretation of election campaigns.

In 1996, a unique professional school of television management was created at the television and radio station Afontovo for the purpose of training television professionals from the Russian regional stations in Krasnoiarsk. The school, known as the Management Center for the Electronic Media, is a public noncommercial organization. More than eighty workers from Russian regional television stations have been trained there in seminars in such fields as general television management and management of the news and sales departments. One of the projects of the center, in March and May 1998, was the holding of two seminars on "Television and Elections." The first seminar, which preceded the election of Lebed' as governor, was intended for the regional stations of the Krasnoiarsk region, a huge territory about ten times the size of Great Britain. Representatives of television stations from different regions of Russia participated in the second seminar, based on the interpretation of this election campaign in the media.

Special attention was paid to such issues as cooperation with public organizations in the regions, which promotes the development of democracy and a civil society in the country; journalistic etiquette; legislation concerning the mass media; and legal aspects of the stations' daily activities. Participation in the seminars by representatives of Tsentrizbirkom (the Central Election Committee, the federal body that organizes and monitors the election), the International Foundation for Election Systems, and the Fund for the Defense of Glasnost'; legal experts; specialists in the area of political agitation; and tv journalists had these aims: to acquaint Russian stations with different methods of interpreting elections on television (an instructional video, "Television in Election Campaigns," was created especially for the seminar); to improve the legal knowledge of the television journalists interpreting the elections and, through their activity, also to improve the legal knowledge of the voters and the organizers of the elections; and to help regional independent television become one of the decisive factors influencing democratic processes in the country, informing the population, and fostering civic action.

At the present time there are several ongoing or planned projects for continuing the training of Russian television journalists. Among them are Internews and BBC projects, as well as various forms of cooperation between journalism departments at Russian and American universities.

The Krasnoiarsk project laid the basis for a truly regional educational center, the Management Center for the Electronic Media. It provides not only theoretical knowledge, but also the possibility of internships in a successfully functioning independent television and radio company. The remoteness of the stations in the Urals, Siberia, and the Far East from the main educational centers of St. Petersburg and Moscow had made it problematic to create a feedback circuit. The geographical position of Krasnoiarsk makes it possible to solve that problem.

In the future an entire network of similar training centers at television stations will probably appear. There are also plans to expand the program of education by organizing seminars and internships in radio station management and in television and radio journalism, and by setting up, on a permanent basis, a School for Advertising Agents to train specialists for the sales departments of regional television stations.

Two of the center's projects in 1997 and 1998 were financed by the Ford, Soros, and Eurasia Foundations. However, the activities of the center have already become self-supporting through a system of providing various services for remuneration: training of television and radio professionals from the countries of the Confederation of Independent States (CIS); consulting services for medium-sized and small regional business on advertising in the mass media; and individual internships for administrative personnel, journalists, and employees of sales departments at independent television and radio stations in Russia and the countries of the CIS.

Conclusion

The facts presented in this report demonstrate that what is occurring in the Russian mass media today, and in the Krasnoiarsk region in particular, is a painful transition from the Soviet model of the press to a radically different model based on the abolition of censorship and on freedom of speech and access to information. The leap from the "land of necessity" to the "land of freedom" cannot be painless, of course. However, judging by what has occurred, I would say the leap obviously has been delayed. The standards of the Russian Constitution and the law "On the Mass Media" do not always coincide with practice in this area, by any means. Censorship, which has a very rich history and powerful traditions in the Russian state, quite often finds a way to remind us of its existence, although it has been officially abolished. On the other hand, journalists themselves, especially those from the young, independent media, sense a need to continue their professional education, inasmuch as the future of freedom in Russia depends to a great extent on how well the media, and television in particular, realize their responsibility as participants in the creation of democratic institutions for the country.

It is already obvious that the programs of the Management Center for the Electronic Media, which received international support in the initial stage and now are based on the participation of both foreign and domestic professionals with teaching skills, will be essential in supporting the development of the growing television industry. And that enables us to look with optimism toward the future of this enigmatic country, a future that is so difficult to predict.

FOREIGN FUNDERS AND RUSSIAN

RECIPIENTS

AREAS OF MISUNDERSTANDING

MIKHAIL KALUZHSKII

Mikhail Kaluzhskii is the executive director of the Novosibirsk branch of the Soros Foundation's Open Society Institute. Formerly a journalist with a special interest in cultural affairs, until 1997 he served as managing director of the Arts and Culture Department of Novaia Sibir', a weekly newspaper in Siberia. Mr. Kaluzhskii is particularly knowledgeable about the cultural obstacles that confront Western foundations and joint projects working to build a civil society in Russia.

WESTERN FOUNDATIONS have been playing an essential role in the development of economic and civil liberties in Russia. I work for one of these foundations, the largest American private charity now active in Russia: the Open Society Institute, better known as the Soros Foundation. I supervise its eastern division, located in Novosibirsk. These figures will illustrate the scope of our work: in 1997 the institute spent $33,091,545 in Russia, about $1.6 million of that amount in Novosibirsk, a region with a population of 2.8 million.

Our sizable organization employs only a few foreigners, all of whom work in the Moscow office. Nevertheless, we use English frequently, both because the institute operates in thirty Eastern European and ex-Soviet countries and needs a lingua franca, and because so much of our paperwork is in English. Mostly, however, my colleagues and I speak daily in a strange tongue, the newspeak of contemporary Russian charity. Our seminars for potential grantees often indicate that our "lingo" is incomprehensible to our applicants.

But how do we correctly translate the words "applicant" and "deadline" into Russian? How do we account for all the nuances of the term "grass roots"? Our Russian-English neologism *allokirovat'* is no better and no worse than *assignovat'*, a word commonly used in modern Russian.

Generally, the great misunderstandings between funders and grantees arise from problems such as these, problems of a lexical nature. But vocabulary is not the only issue; we also are involved in "translating" abstract ideas from one culture to another. And there are many ways in which the funders and the recipients fail to understand one another. I can safely generalize here, because the Western foundations operating in Russia are alike in many respects. Foreign charities have many different programs in Russia, but all of them – with the possible exception of foundations for the natural sciences – declare support for the institutions of a civil society. Almost 100 percent of their support is directed at nongovernment organizations, NGOs, also known as the third sector. But what precisely do westerners support when they assist Russian NGOs? Do the funders take into account the differences in culture? Do they believe that civil society and the third sector are identical?

First, confusion ensues when one seeks an adequate equivalent for the term "nongovernment organization." Of course, words like *nepravitel'stvennaia* or, better yet, *negosudarstvennaia organizatsiia* are acceptable. Such terminology is not used in the Russian legislature, however, and thus "NGO" is commonly rendered as *nekommercheskaia* (noncommercial), or *obshchestvennaia organizatsiia* (public organization), or *tretii sektor* (the third sector). The adjective *nekommercheskaia* is more common. Here, problems of language are secondary to issues of law and culture. For Russians, "government" is not the state authority in general, but the current regime. The theory of three sectors, according to which a developed democracy has three distinct parts – the government, private profit, and private nonprofit sectors – becomes inadequate as soon as the terms are translated. Nor can this theory be applied indiscriminately to Russia.

In speaking of the United States, Alexis de Tocqueville noted the importance of NGOS in public life in 1835: "While a new cause is headed by the government in France, and by aristocracy in England, in the United States you will be sure to find an association or a union." At about the same time, the Russian writer Petr Viazemskii observed, "In Russia, there is no society, only population." Only in the 1860s, after a period of reform, did the first public organizations arise. These associations and charities – some four thousand at the turn of the century – assisted in the development of a civil society in late nineteenth-century Russia, but all such efforts came to a standstill in 1917.

Though the Communists destroyed the roots of civil society in Russia and so perverted the very notion of volunteerism that most people, even today, associate it with hard, unpaid labor, fairness demands that I point out that NGOS existed legally in the Soviet Union. The decree of the Central Executive Committee of the Council of People's Commissars of January 6, 1930, "On Establishment and Liquidation of National Nonprofit Societies and Unions" and the memorandum of July 10, 1932, "On Voluntary Societies and Unions" allowed the functioning of NGOS such as trade unions and the Academy of Sciences.

Naturally, their existence did not facilitate the development of a civil society; in fact, it often achieved the opposite. The elements of a civil society in the Soviet Union could exist only illegally. Formally, however, the Soviet NGOS perfectly fit the definition of the third sector as legally registered, nongovernment, nonprofit, self-governed voluntary organizations serving the interests of the public. In actuality they were – and the Academy of Sciences still largely remains – government organizations or institutions in opposition to a civil society, functioning as part of the state machinery for manipulating the public.

The meaning of the word "governmental" is not easy to convey because of cultural differences. While the distinctions between national, regional, state, and municipal government levels make sense in the United States, they still are largely irrelevant in Russia, especially as far as regions are concerned. For the general public in Russia, the distinction between nongovernmental and governmental, with the latter including federal, *oblast'*, and municipal levels and the former including both private and public, remains more significant. Incidentally, this misunderstanding is responsible for the prevailing skepticism regarding NGOs. The notion of what is truly "governmental" is blurred by local administrations, for example. In some regions, heads of local administrations are appointed by governors, rather than elected.

Terminological confusion prevails in regard to other features of a civil society: gender politics, for example. Czech philosopher Jirina Siklova, in her characteristically titled article "Why We Resist Western-style Feminism," writes: "Discussions of Western feminists about whether women are a social class and whether sexual or social inequality is primary appear meaningless." Such meaninglessness has both historical and contemporary origins. Western feminists are primarily concerned with issues of employment, domestic violence, and sexist symbolism in the media. In Eastern Europe, according to Siklova, women do not identify their social and economic problems with gender or sexual discrimination. In socialist countries, almost all employable women are employed, thus bearing the double burden of career and housework. "Women who have survived 'real socialism' believe that Western feminists overestimate the significance of employment for emancipation," says Siklova.

This is just another example of the troubles caused by miscommunication. In the case of the "third sector," the misunderstanding is due to the fact that the theory of three sectors did not originate naturally in Russia. Moreover, even the notion of developing a civil society in Russia is itself artificial. According to Natalia Varlamova, a Russian legal expert, "while traditionally civil society formed beyond government, finding a niche free of state power, in Russia today it is being cultivated by the government, which dooms the end result."

Since the beginning of democratic reform in Russia, the government has acted as a fair distributor of political and civil liberties, voluntarily relinquishing some of its own powers. A civil society can exist only in a law-abiding state. However, as Hungarian political scientist Andras Sajo reminds us, laws always serve the establishment and preserve the status quo. The government provided opportunities for civic initiatives by setting up a legal framework that still is not properly used in Russia. I refer to the laws "On Public Associations," passed by the Duma on April 14, 1995, "On Charity and Charitable Organizations," passed on July 7, 1995, and "On Nonprofit Organizations," passed on December 8, 1995.

It is only natural that foreign governments, charities, and even citizens acted as godparents to the third sector in Russia. Sometimes their well-intended efforts did not take into account local specifics, and in some cases they evoked a nationalistic response. In "Universal Rights, Missionaries, Converts, and 'Local Savages': The Drawbacks of Western Aid to Legal Reform," Sajo, the political scientist quoted above, says, "To achieve results, the developers of legal reforms should have started with analyzing the readiness of Eastern Europe for human rights reforms. Otherwise, they are doomed to make pointless approaches, led by vague believers in unclear ideals, or to formally replicate Western practices, making substitutions for the values they are supposed to serve. When a fetish become a religion, the religion is likely to become a ritual."

Often, Western methods and ideas were wholly new to Russians. Sarah Lindemann, an American who was one of the founders of the Siberian Center for the Support of Civic Initiatives, an NGO resource clearinghouse, remembers: "When the center started in April 1995, the third, or NGO nonprofit, sector was virtually nonexistent." Where there is wholesale innovation, there is ample scope for misunderstanding.

Not long ago, an NGO from one of Siberia's largest cities applied to the Novosibirsk Open Society Institute for support. This organization employs both Americans and Russians in a school-based community center project. Half the project had been funded by a large private American foundation, and the organization sought matching funds from us. From a formal point of view, this project should have been approved for the grant, but it was rejected. Why did one foundation offer support, while another refused it? Many of the project's ideas were interesting, but both our experts and our advisory board disliked one of its key features: cooperation between the school and the community was becoming so close that changes in the school curriculum were in the offing. To the American developers and funders, that step seemed perfectly natural, but to the Russian experts at the Open Society Institute in Novosibirsk, it was completely unacceptable.

From the Russian experts' point of view, the project seemed artificial. Their verdict, I believe, has to do with the overall artificiality of the practices employed to create a third sector in Russia. In this situation, exclusive support of the third sector can play a negative role by reinforcing the stereotypical belief that only certain types of organizations can obtain Western funding. A change in the funders' strategy would allow the grantees to diversify their efforts. Otherwise, it may become a meaningless pumping of money from Western funders into Russian NGOs. Unfortunately, Russia already has a class of professional fundraisers, for whom obtaining money is more important than promoting civic initiatives.

As for cooperation between the sectors, contacts are limited to government and to businesses that support the third sector. There is no mutual cooperation, because NGOs neither manufacture goods nor provide services. In the United States the third sector represents 10 percent of the job market; it makes its presence felt in the national economy. In Russia the third sector plays no such role. Laws regulating relations between NGOs and the government are virtually nonexistent, especially at the local level. Moreover, the existing laws cannot ensure the necessary transparency and competitiveness, since they require numerous additional regulatory acts. Besides, governments often view NGOs from a political angle, a tendency that is particularly significant now, as elections for the Duma and the presidency near.

Having described some of the limitations of an exclusive approach to third-sector support in Russia, I would like to mention some of the success stories. The Open Society Institute, for example, finds satisfactory ways of promoting a civil society in Russia through its support of various institutions. The Siberian Center for Support of Civic Initiatives, set up almost from scratch by American enthusiasts in 1995, is another example. This organization, with its powerful network of eleven resource centers in the largest cities of Siberia – from Tiumen' in the east to Chita in the west, a distance roughly equal to that between Seattle and Chicago – conducts seven different programs for Siberian NGOs and provides training, workshops, legal and financial assistance, Internet access, and printing facilities. What is the source of its funding? The money comes primarily from the West, of course. But I am convinced that the center's success is due not only to its good relations with Western funders, but also to its cooperation with local government and business. Thus the center can rely on local resources; moreover, it has set a precedent for cooperation among the sectors. For the center, working with local businesses does not mean merely asking for $50 to buy paper for a single mother's organization; it entails a comprehensive program of consciousness-raising designed to educate the local business community about the role of corporate charity as a marketing tool. The center's experience demonstrates that cooperation among the three sectors not only promotes NGO sustainability, but creates a real instrument for developing a civil society.

We constantly observe instances in which intersector cooperation is realized within the institutions that have been the most influential arena of socialization in Russia: education, the mass media, and the cultural sphere. I will focus on the cultural sphere, since it bears a direct relation to my own work. In fact, if I am not mistaken, the Open Society Institute is the only private foundation in Russia that supports Russian culture, especially the arts.

From the standpoint of the theory of the three sectors, it seems extravagant to view cultural institutions as a tool of civic development. In the Soviet Union, cultural organizations were predominantly governmental, especially at the regional level. It is pointless to compare this state of affairs with the situation in the United States;

let me just note that there are American cultural organizations in all three sectors. The Library of Congress, for example, is in the government sector. Russians and Americans differ, too, in their notions of what constitutes "culture."

Practically all Russian cultural institutions are governmental; most attempts to set up private galleries or theaters in the country's outlying regions have failed for financial reasons. Let me add that in Russia today, the term "governmental" needs clarification; one has to differentiate between "belonging to the government" and "funded by the government." Cultural organizations are only formally governmental, but their managers put them in the position of acting as either "nongovernmental" or "nonprofit" organizations.

Though comparisons between Russian and American cultural organizations miss the point, the Russian situation can be compared with that in other countries where the government traditionally administers culture. Here too, Russian organizations fail to fit the accepted definition of "governmental." It is difficult to imagine, for example, that a German state theater would rent its facilities, equipment, and costumes; try to start a printing business; organize dancing classes and charge for participation; and offer its premises for parties, auctions, and fashion shows, yet be unable to produce a play without sponsorship, because government funds cover only salaries and utilities. The salaries are low and never paid on time, and the funds for payment of utilities often take the form of illiquid securities. Imagine, at the same time, that such a theater would apply to foreign foundations for funds to retrain managers and create a theatergoers' NGO so as to have a good image and a stable box office. These and similar things are true of dozens of Russian theaters, museums, and libraries that have different sources of funds and use different marketing strategies. How could they behave otherwise, in light of the lack of stable government funding and the absence of a well-thought-out cultural policy in the official realm? The situation reminds me of what Alla Solovieva, a St. Petersburg sociologist, once said: "In Russia, the third sector is the nonindustrial sector." The theory of the three sectors has to be amended to fit Russian circumstances: "Nonprofit" is not necessarily "nongovernmental."

In conclusion, I want to suggest that creating a civil society in Russia is impossible if it is to be achieved through support of the third sector. Among the impediments to success are the nonprofit, multisectoral nature of Russian cultural institutions and the traditional role of the arts in socialization, established in part under the Soviet regime. Two more plausible means to the end of a civil society are the support of joint efforts by government, business, and the public sector, perhaps with special emphasis on cooperation between NGOs and business, and the support of Russian culture. Any organization that plans to provide assistance to Russia, or any other country, has to acquaint itself with the specifics of the culture and consider the opinions of local experts.

PART IV

ADVANCING FREEDOM OF INQUIRY AND BELIEF

ADVANCING FREEDOM

OF BELIEF IN RUSSIA

LAWRENCE A. UZZELL

From 1995 to 1999, Lawrence Uzzell was the Moscow representative of the Keston Institute, an Oxford-based interconfessional organization that monitors freedom of religion and researches religious affairs in communist and postcommunist countries. Now director of Keston, Mr. Uzzell recently was nominated for a Pulitzer Prize for his reportage on Russia's 1997 law restoring state control over religious life.

THE KESTON INSTITUTE was begun by Michael Bourdeaux, who spent a year in Moscow in the late 1950s as part of the first wave of British exchange students. During his stay he walked the city's streets and counted churches, because that was the only way to learn how many Russian Orthodox churches were still open and functioning. As it turned out, there were about forty-one, and this was the first reliable count available to us in the West. Before 1917, the number was more than 1,600. Michael decided then to make it his life's work to be the voice of the voiceless, the advocate of the persecuted of all religious faiths in the Soviet Union, and he set up the Keston Institute for that purpose.

I became part of the Keston organization fairly recently. Ten years ago I was a journalist in Washington, D.C., reporting exclusively on domestic American politics, especially education policy. Russia seemed to me then to be the most interesting country in the world, and in my effort to learn more about it I became a reader of the material published by the Keston Institute. I began to organize members of my own church parish in Bethesda, Maryland, to write letters to prisoners of conscience about whom we learned from the Keston materials. We knew that such letters would make a great difference to the well-being of their authors, even if they never reached their destination.

About eight or nine years ago, at an Orthodox church in Washington, I met Father Georgii Edel'shtein, who was introduced to me by Father Viktor Potopov, a Voice of America broadcaster and a local Orthodox priest. This encounter reinforced my wish to move to Moscow, to live and work in Russia. I finally had the chance in 1992, when I joined a secular American think tank that studies Russian politics and economics. I continued to do volunteer work for Keston, which had been declared an enemy of the Soviet state and was on the KGB's short list of institutions that were to be kept out of Russia if possible. Not until 1992 was the Keston Institute able to open a small Moscow office with, initially, a part-time staff. In 1995, Keston decided to hire a full-time Moscow representative, and I threw my hat into the ring.

What most attracts me about the Keston Institute – though my view may seem unpatriotic – is its very British style. Keston combines a passionate commitment to freedom with an extremely understated, judicious, and balanced approach that reflects Michael Bourdeaux's distinctive personal manner. I like to describe this style as "Anglican jihad."

Since Keston is an interconfessional organization, we have people on our staff who represent all forms of Christianity, and we defend the rights of Muslims, Buddhists, and members of other faiths as well. I like to think of myself as a personal symbol of Keston's tolerance and nondiscriminatory policies, not so much because the institute chose an American to succeed its founder as because Michael Bourdeaux, a canon of the Diocese of Rochester in the Church of England, decided that he wanted as his successor an "apostate," a former member of his own Anglican Communion. Previously an Episcopalian, I converted to Orthodox Christianity twenty years ago. Now I am in the position of regularly pointing a finger at bishops of my own church – the church in which I receive the sacrament on Sundays – for their violations of the rights of other faiths.

I'm often asked what it feels like to be a Russian Orthodox Christian defending Catholics, Protestants, and other religious minorities in Russia. My motivation, I believe, is even stronger than that of my Catholic and Protestant colleagues. They worry about protecting Catholics and Protestants from persecution; I worry about the souls of my coreligionists. My chief concern is that my fellow Orthodox Christians not become persecutors, and that, I think, is more important in the long run. Ultimately it is far worse to be a persecutor than to be a victim of persecution.

In keeping with Keston's British style, I now want to say something that may surprise those of you who are used to hearing human rights advocates exaggerate the threats facing their constituencies: There is virtually no religious persecution in Russia today, not in the proper sense of that term. True persecution unquestionably does exist in China, Saudi Arabia, and the Sudan. But if religious persecution means entering people's homes and arresting them just for reading the Bible, if it means holding prisoners of conscience in labor camps just because of their religious activities, then there is no religious persecution in Russia today, though it did exist in the Soviet Union as recently as fifteen years ago.

What Russia has today is religious repression, and this phenomenon is on the rise. The state is creating more and more barriers to religious minorities, especially Protestants, who want to observe their faith in public, not only behind the closed doors of their own apartments. Religious repression will continue to grow for at least the next several years.

Religious discrimination is also pervasive, especially in relations with the military and with other state agencies; it is reflected in state subsidies and other forms of state favoritism at the expense of the non-Orthodox. The Russian Orthodox Church has emerged as a de facto state church, an established church. From the standpoint of human rights, this discrimination may not be alarming. Many Western European countries, such as Norway, have established churches that receive state subsidies while at the same time granting religious minorities full freedom of worship and practice. What is important here, however, is the fact that the Russian Constitution, passed in 1993, states clearly that Russia respects the principle of separation of church and state, that there is no state church in Russia, and that all religious associations are equal before the law. That is a strong statement, stronger than any corresponding statement in the U.S. Constitution. The phrase "all religious associations" means not just that Judaism and Christianity, for example, are equal before the law, but that every Jewish synagogue, every Christian parish, is equal to every other congregation in its relations with the state. Unfortunately theory and practice are at variance here: Russia now is grossly violating that principle of its own Constitution.

Religious freedom grew steadily in Russia from about the mid-1980s to approximately 1993. We now are observing the fifth anniversary of the all-time peak of religious freedom in Russia, not only in theory but also in practice. In late 1993 and early 1994, the new Constitution, with its splendid provisions for religious freedom, was enacted. Unfashionable religious minorities of all kinds had more opportunity than ever before or since to practice their faith publicly without being harassed by the police, being told to take their banners down and go elsewhere, or having their brochures confiscated on the street. I suggest that the concurrence of these legal and practical peaks was largely happenstance.

The real religious freedom that existed in practice was not a by-product of the 1993 Constitution, nor of the conversion of Russia's political elite to belief in Western principles of freedom, but rather a result of the turmoil and chaos of the early 1990s, which prevented the Russian elite from keeping a steady hand on things. That hand is firmer now, and there has been a steady deterioration of religious freedom over the past five years. In 1994, the first provincial law restricting the rights of religious minorities was passed, in Tula, about two hundred miles south of Moscow. About one-third of Russia's provinces have passed similar laws since then, and in 1997 the national government passed a law explicitly distinguishing between first-class "religious organizations" and second-class "religious groups," which have far fewer rights.

The 1997 law differentiates between those congregations that are over fifteen years old and had good relations with the Soviet state and those that are less than fifteen years old. If this law is strictly enforced, congregations in the latter category would lack such basic rights as the right to publish religious literature or to engage in educational activities. I predict that as this law is applied in practice, as the local provincial bureaucracies learn more about its provisions, the situation will continue to deteriorate for at least the next two years. Anyone who ventures to make longer-term projections than that is either much smarter or much more foolhardy than I. Fortunately this law, so harsh on paper, has actually been implemented in a much milder way in most provinces. Indeed, the harshest violations of religious freedom now have to do with things that are not explicit in the text of the 1997 law. They are, in fact, violations both of that law and of the more tolerant law of 1990, which it replaced.

According to Justice Scalia, economic freedom is not distinct from human rights; economic freedoms and other forms of freedom are inseparable. In Russia today, the most common violations of religious freedom are occurring in precisely those areas where economic freedom and religious freedom intersect. If Russia did not still have a largely socialist pattern of property ownership, these violations would be much more difficult for the bureaucrats to commit. Most real estate in the typical Russian provincial city, for example, is owned either by the city or by the provincial government. In fewer cases, the federal government is the owner. Thus almost any place in which a medium-sized or large gathering, be it religious or secular in nature, could be held is state-owned. The local movie theater, the equivalent of the YMCA hall, or almost any other room larger than a private apartment can be appointed as a meeting place only with the bureaucracy's permission. In the Russia of today, still in transition, these state-owned buildings are rented on a commercial basis to anyone with sufficient funds: the local chess club, the local atheist club, computer exhibitors, schools teaching English for businessmen. Rental of such places to religious bodies was common in the early 1990s, but more recently a crackdown has been evident at the local level. More frequently, local bureau-crats have been telling members of religious minorities – especially Protestants – that a religious service can be held in such a venue only with the permission of the local Orthodox priest. This asser-tion directly violates the constitutional and legal principle that there is to be no state church in Russia.

Roman Catholics usually do not rent such places, but they have their own problems with real estate. Within the borders of the Rus-sian Federation, there are as many as one million Russian citizens of Catholic ancestry. Before 1917 there were about three hundred Catholic parishes within the borders of what is now the Russian Federation. To an American visiting provincial Russia, it is striking that in places like Irkutsk in the depths of Siberia and in other places one would think of as exclusively Orthodox, one finds neo-Gothic, Western-style Roman Catholic church buildings, which were built by and for the local population of ethnic Poles in the nineteenth century. Many such buildings are still standing, though the Soviet regime seized and forcibly secularized them, along with most Or-thodox church buildings. The post-Soviet state has returned some of these churches for use by newly revived Catholic parishes, but many are still in the hands of the state. During the past few years the authorities have been increasingly reluctant to return Catholic church buildings to their rightful owners. There has been no progress whatsoever in Catholics' efforts to recover the Church of St. Peter and St. Paul in Moscow, though efforts to recover the Church of the Immaculate Conception, also in Moscow, proved successful because the Catholics started sooner and pushed harder. The latter campaign began in the late 1980s and succeeded only in 1996; if it were just beginning today, it probably would fail.

To be fair, I should mention that the Orthodox often have the same problem. If an Orthodox church building happens to be oc-cupied by a secular institution that enjoys good political relations with the local authorities, the Orthodox bishop may lose the battle to recover his diocese's rightful property. The difference, of course, is that the Orthodox clergy often have good political connections of their own, much better than those of the Roman Catholics. In both cases, however, believers are fighting battles that they should not have to fight. And if the state were not still deeply imbued with socialist views of property ownership, they would not have to fight them.

One revealing indication of the real significance of the 1997 law is the state's treatment of the Old Believers. This confession, probably the most distinctively Russian form of Christianity, resulted from a schism within the Russian Orthodox Church in the seventeenth century. It exists only in Russia and in places to which it has been brought by Russian émigrés. If the 1997 law were, as its supporters claim, a defense of Russia's traditional religions against exotic alien newcomers such as the Hare Krishna sect or the Mormons, then the Old Believers would have no problems under the new legislation. But they are having considerable problems. In summer 1997, when the Catholics and the Baptists were hesitating, it was Metropolitan Alimpii of the Old Believers who refused to make any compromises regarding the newly proposed law, because he sensed that it would be a continuation of the age-old policy of trampling on the Old Believers, a policy embraced both by pre-Soviet Russia and by the Soviet state.

Many of you have been to Moscow; all of you, I hope, will go there someday. When you visit Red Square, one of the inspiring sights you will see opposite the Kremlin, near the GUM department store, is the Kazan' Cathedral, a triumph of architectural restoration. This seventeenth-century structure was razed under Stalin because it blocked the incessant parades of tanks and military might that Stalin liked to hold in Red Square. Though the cathedral was destroyed down to its last brick, Russian architectural historians had detailed plans of the building, and it has been rebuilt faithfully, in its entirety. The last stone was set in 1993. The dark side of this story is that the Kazan' Cathedral has a tower in which there hangs a piece of stolen property, a bell that originally belonged to the Old Believers. A wealthy merchant family donated it to the largest Old Believer cathedral in Moscow at the beginning of the twentieth century. It was confiscated by the Soviet state and kept in storage for many decades. In 1993, under the post-Soviet regime, it was finally "returned" – not to its rightful owners but to the mainstream Russian Orthodox Church. Both church and state officials now refuse to correct this injustice.

The bell in the Kazan' Cathedral is only one of many hundreds of pieces of stolen Old Believer property that ended up in the hands of the mainstream Moscow Patriarchate. Other items include icons stolen by ordinary criminals from Old Believer churches, then intercepted by the border guards or the city police, and later "returned" to the Moscow Patriarchate. The Old Believers wanted the 1997 law to include a provision requiring that whenever a piece of stolen church property is to be returned, it first should be independently reviewed by experts who can determine what confession is the rightful recipient. The Moscow Patriarchate rejected this proposed amendment.

Those who are suffering under the 1997 law clearly include people whose credentials as members of an age-old Russian faith cannot be in doubt. Even more ironic is the fact that American missionaries in Russia have suffered relatively little under this law. It would be immensely difficult, though not quite impossible, to find specific cases of American Protestant missionaries – about whom such an uproar has been made – whose lives are markedly worse today than they were three years ago, when the law was passed. But it is not at all difficult to find indigenous Russian Protestants whose lives this law has made worse. Ignoring the text of its own 1997 law, the Yeltsin administration is observing an old Russian practice: Roll out the red carpet for foreigners, but treat your own people like dirt.

This law threatens not only Protestants, but independent Muslims as well. The greatest single violation of religious freedom in Russia last year involved Muslims. It took place in Kazan', the capital of the Republic of Tatarstan, which is composed almost equally of Tatars, whose ancestors traditionally were Muslim, and Slavs, whose ancestors were Orthodox. The president of the republic decided that the mufti, the head of the Tatarstan spiritual directorate for Muslims, was too independent of mind. The mufti and the president had already clashed many times over the republic's failure to return mosques and other items of Muslim religious property. The president immediately organized a campaign against the mufti. His administration told the local imams – the heads of Islamic congregations – that if they wanted to continue receiving subsidies for heating and electricity for their buildings, if they wanted the state to cover the costs of their trip to Kazan' for the congress at which the next mufti would be elected, they would vote "the right way" at that congress. And he succeeded, with this combination of carrots and sticks, in replacing the independent-minded mufti with a puppet. That story has not received much coverage in the Western press, though it would have been widely publicized if it had involved a Catholic or Protestant or Jewish religious leader, I am certain.

Another element deserving attention is the re-emergence of the Council for Religious Affairs. One of the most striking things I experience on my visits to provincial, rural Russia is this: Whenever I go to a new provincial capital, I ask, "Who is the *upolnomochennyi*, the plenipotentiary?" Everyone immediately knows whom I mean. The person's formal title usually is not *upolnomochennyi*, but something like "advisor to the provincial governor on cooperation with religious organizations." *Upolnomochennyi* was the title used by provincial officials fifteen years ago, in the old structure called the *Sovet po delam religii*, the Council for Religious Affairs, the mission of which was to regulate religious life in the interests of the atheist state. About half the time when I visit a provincial capital, I find that the local official in charge of church-state relations is the very same person who ten or fifteen years ago was the local *upolnomochennyi* of the Council for Religious Affairs. The same networks reappear under different names.

The picture is not all black and white, however. Some local officials use their positions to work for tolerance and freedom and to establish good relations between majority and minority confessions. Some do not. Real variety of attitude is evident in the provinces, not just in religious life but in other areas as well. It is a striking phenomenon: the real action is now occurring in the provinces. In some provinces, the situation is even worse than one would expect from reading the formal text of the laws. Other provinces are genuine islands of freedom. One such example is Samara, in the Volga valley, where relations between the local Orthodox bishop and the local Catholic priest are excellent. The governor there is pursuing a policy of real tolerance.

It has been suggested that the notion that "small is beautiful" may not be correct in Russia. It is usually the case in Russia that transferring power from Moscow to the provinces means transferring power from relatively more pro-reform to relatively less pro-reform leaders, though that statement may not be as accurate today as it was six months ago. But I suggest that even if it is true, in the long run the transfer of power to provincial leaders is a good thing. It is good because we do not know of any example in history in which a geographic area the size of Russia or North America has been governed as a free polity without being organized as some type of decentralized federation.

And decentralization is now taking place. It may be taking place in a wild, bandit-like fashion, violating Russia's own laws and Constitution, but it is actually taking place. In some places that means an immediate change for the better. In all places, I believe, it gives Russians a chance to learn from their own experiences. That is going to matter more than any amount of preaching or browbeating by us in the West. Russians are going to learn from the comparative experience of those provinces that employ police-state methods against religious minorities and those that do not. One thing they will learn is that the spiritual life of the Orthodox Church is healthier in those provinces that do not use means of naked repression against religious minorities. In the long run that may be all it takes.

When I go to the provinces and talk to simple Russian Orthodox believers, I do not find that they are clamoring for the use of repressive methods against religious minorities. More typical is the Orthodox grandmother, or *babushka,* whom I met in the city of Briansk near the Ukrainian border. Briansk is one of those cities with a nineteenth-century Catholic church. The Catholics now have revived their parish and are trying to get their church building back, but the local authorities argue that there never was a Catholic parish in Briansk, despite the tangible proof to the contrary. The old church is now being used as an apartment building. One of the apartments in it is the home of a pious old Russian Orthodox woman who has befriended the revived Catholic parish. At her invitation, a Roman Catholic mass now is held every month in her apartment, in what long was a Catholic place of worship. This Orthodox *babushka*, I believe, represents the future of Russia.

THE ORTHODOX RUSSIAN

CHURCH ISSUES OF OUR TIMES

FATHER GEORGII EDEL'SHTEIN

Father Georgii Edel'shtein is a dedicated human rights activist in Russia. In 1956, one year after his baptism, he began a twenty-two-year struggle to receive approval for ordination. For many of his twenty years as a priest, he was refused permission to say mass because he insisted on preaching and catechizing. He now has his own parish church in the diocese of Kostroma, where he is engaged in spiritual and social work. As part of that work, Father Edel'shtein takes care of a group of destitute ex-convicts who turned to him for help. In this chapter he focuses on the Moscow Patriarchate, the "most reactionary institution in Russia."

I PREFER NOT TO USE the term "Russian Orthodox Church"; that designation is a creation of Soviet newspeak. In all official state documents our church has always been called the Orthodox Russian Church, and so it should remain for all time. Over seventy years ago the Orthodox Russian Church broke up into several parts, which have not had eucharistic relations all these years. This grave spiritual illness, the division of our church, persists to this day. Under the Soviet regime we excused our common sin with references to external circumstances independent of us, and to heavy-handed interference in the inner life of the church by the state, controlled by militant atheists. Today we no longer have those circuitous excuses; the guilt is ours alone.

The Moscow Patriarchate, which since the Stalinist era has been known officially as the "Russian Orthodox Church," is only one of the parts of the Orthodox Russian Church. The issue of the number of those parts and their interrelations is beyond the scope of this chapter, of course. I only wish to emphasize that I am not imagining a future free and democratic Russia, whatever its political structure might be, without the active participation of a united Orthodox Russian Church – restored in accordance with the decisions of the All-Russian Church Council of 1917 and 1918 – in all spheres of the country's life.

This chapter is the fruit not of dispassionate academic studies but of twenty years of experience in church service in village parishes of the Kursk-Belgorod, Vologda, and Kostroma dioceses, and of many years of agonized reflection about the course and the future of the Orthodox Church in Russia. Like all personal experience, it inevitably contains subjective evaluations and biases and is not free from error.

I have deliberately concentrated on that branch of the church in which I myself serve – the Moscow Patriarchate – because, like any other Christian, I remember the Savior's command: "First take the log out of your own eye, and then you will see clearly to take the speck out of your brother's eye" (Matt. 7:5).

Twelve years ago, on April 29, 1988, the then-General Secretary of the Central Committee of the Communist Party of the Soviet Union (CPSU), Mikhail Gorbachev, met in the Kremlin with Patriarch Pimen and the permanent members of the Holy Synod and had a protracted discussion with them. It is customary to consider that the cornerstone of epoch-making transformations in the Moscow Patriarchate was laid on that day. After that, the patriarchate ostensibly was miraculously revived and transformed.

"The rebirth and return to health of the Orthodox Church in Russia is at hand! . . . The passage of the new law to a significant extent strengthens the independence of the church! . . . This is a blessed, miraculous turning point in the history of Russian Orthodoxy," according to *Vestnik Rossiiskogo Khristianskogo Dvizheniia* (the Journal of the Russian Christian Movement) in 1990. "The Russian church, in two or three years of *glasnost'* (which for the church began only in 1988), has already achieved independence in its relations with the state."

Glasnost' exists only in our state, however; in the Moscow Patriarchate there is no more *glasnost'* now than there was fifteen or twenty years ago. The patriarchate is an exceptional, highly secretive institution, the most reactionary institution in Russia. All these years it has managed not to publish a single secret document from its archives; it has managed not to speak a single word of truth about its sixty-year past, about its interrelations with the Ideological Department of the Central Committee of the CPSU, with the KGB, and with the Council for Religious Affairs, which is affiliated with the Council of Ministers of the USSR. It is shameful that today the Cheka-GPU-KGB (which, it seems, has in its turn been renamed) is a more open and truthful institution than the Moscow Patriarchate. Even nine years ago KGB General Oleg Kalugin officially stated that his "office" had always appointed the top authorities of the religious organizations. On October 31, 1991, the newspaper *Izvestia* wrote: "General Nikolai Stoliarov confirmed the affiliation of the former Council for Religious Affairs and of several priests with the KGB. He reported the existence of a church supervisory department within the structure of the Ideological Department of the KGB." Then dozens of documents about the secret collaboration of the chief hierarchs of the Moscow Patriarchate with the KGB were published, but the Holy Synod remains silent.

Before the meeting of General Secretary Gorbachev with members of the Synod, streams of slander and disinformation about the position of the church and believers in Russia flowed like huge, deep rivers. The disinformation was spread by all the media of mass communication, by the officials of the Council for Religious Affairs, by the hierarchs of the Moscow Patriarchate, and by numerous delegates and guests at "peace forums" and other representatives of "progressive world society." However, a small counter-flow – officially titled "libelous bourgeois propaganda" or "bourgeois falsification of the situation of believers in the USSR" – has continued all these years.

After the historic meeting of April 29, 1988, and especially after the ostentatious celebration of the millennium of Russia's conversion to Christianity, false witness and disinformation spilled over, throughout the entire world, into a boundless ocean. The counter-flow of objective information that issued from various "dissidents" dried up into a little brook and was almost completely lost in the immense ocean of hysterical behavior and pseudo-religious propaganda. The river of academic research by foreign specialists reversed course and began to flow backwards, cutting a new channel for its waters almost parallel to the channel of Communist political agitation and *Zhurnal Moskovskoi Patriarkhii* (the Journal of the Moscow Patriarchate). To be convinced of that, it is sufficient to turn the pages of the publication I mentioned earlier: the highly authoritative, widely disseminated *Vestnik Rossiiskogo Khristianskogo Dvizheniia,* published in Paris and Moscow. Over the last ten years, *Vestnik* has not published a single document concerning the ties of the chief hierarchs of the Moscow Patriarchate with the KGB, not a single document about Archbishop Ermogen (Golubev), the priest Nikolai Eshliman, or the confessor Boris Talantov.

Thirty-six years ago, in 1964, when a letter from the priests Nikolai Eshliman and Gleb Iakunin to Patriarch Aleksii (Simanskii) was published in *samizdat,* the editor-in-chief of *Vestnik* wrote in an editorial: "For some forty years now, since the time of the Sergiev Declaration, the church, in the person of its own official representatives, has denied truth and humanity. This denial led to a profound moral decline, slander about the martyrs, and endless glorification of Stalin. And then, when internal corruption had begun to threaten the very existence of the church, the courageous and truthful voice of the two priests was heard. All at once, mystically, the entire essence of the church has changed. The words of the two priests have become a dividing sword. From now on a lie cannot be dressed up as the truth, or faint-heartedness as a perceptive estimate."

Alas, today, the lie of the Moscow Patriarchate is once again being dressed up as the truth. After the August putsch of 1991, a special Commission of the Supreme Soviet was created to investigate the causes and circumstances of the GKChP.[1] For a very short time the members of the commission were granted access to a portion of

1. The GKChP (*gosudarstvennyi komitet po chrezvychainomu polozheniiu* = state committee on the state of emergency) was the self-styled "emergency committee" that attempted the unsuccessful August 1991 coup against Gorbachev; by extension, the acronym refers here to the attempted coup as a whole.

the secret documents. Those documents indisputably confirmed that all the chief hierarchs of the patriarchate willingly cooperated with the KGB and were secret agents with twenty to thirty years of service.

The documents were published, but nobody in the world was seriously interested in them; I dare say that no one even paid attention to this unique situation: *all* the chief hierarchs were collaborators with the secret police, *all* of them were active accomplices of the diabolical regime, little wheels and screws in the mechanism of the totalitarian state of militant atheists.

The U.S. Library of Congress invited the leaders of the Commission of the Supreme Soviet, Lev Ponomarev and Gleb Iakunin, to Washington, but even after that nobody was interested in the documents. To this day not one of the secret agents has confessed; more than nine years have passed, but all the collaborators, as before, occupy the same chairs and the same administrative posts. As before, they meet with their brothers in Christ, whom for many years they handed over and betrayed and against whom they wrote secret denunciations. Those who earned their living in the profession of Judas continue to give a brotherly kiss, both at home and abroad, and unblushingly repeat: "Christ is among us. He is and will remain."

Long ago three singularly talented artists were ordered to paint a portrait of a terrible ruler who had one eye, a withered arm, and a crippled leg. The first artist painted him just as he was and was severely punished for having attempted to betray the fearful secret and tempt the ordinary citizens. The second depicted the sovereign with two healthy arms and legs, and he was also punished for attempting to raise doubts in the minds of his fellow citizens. And the third portrayed the ruler in profile. The bad eye was concealed, the withered arm was covered by a shield, the crippled leg was hidden by the horse's hindquarters. The basic principle of all those who speak and write about the Moscow Patriarchate today is to portray it "in profile," that is, never to lie directly, as far as possible, or to fabricate, but to avoid speaking the truth in every case and to conceal the lame leg, the withered arm, and the bad eye from the ordinary folk.

We have gone lame and lost an eye from the friendly embraces of Communist power, but we do not cry out to the Physician with a prayer for healing. Instead, as before, we remain chained to the source of infection. More and more documentary films, articles, lectures, interviews, and reports from church councils cheerfully testify that in Russia new parishes are being opened and religious literature is being distributed, that libraries and almshouses are being organized, but they are stubbornly silent about these facts: We, the members of the clergy, are systematically robbing our own parishioners; our entire administration has become steeped in corruption; and the religious literature that was presented to us free of charge from all over the world was sold at very high prices, and no one from outside knows to where the proceeds vanished. The impoverished village churches have not received a cent of that money.

The hierarchs of the Moscow Patriarchate don't care how the money is made: it never has an odor. They made it on children's Bibles and on three-volume explanatory Bibles. Then they started to make money on duty-free imports of millions of cigarettes, on alcoholic beverages, on chicken legs – "Bush legs," as they are generally known in Russia – on "Holy Spring" water, and on diamonds and oil.

Without the slightest reverence, Canadian professor D. Pospelovskii, a well-known specialist in the history of the Orthodox Russian Church and one of the most consistent and indefatigable apologists for the Moscow Patriarchate, wrote in *Vestnik* in 1990 about the terrible procedures prevailing in the patriarchate even in the years of so-called *perestroika* and *glasnost'*: "In the past decade, when the late Patriarch Pimen to all intents and purposes was no longer on the job, the church was run in his name by the favorites who surrounded the patriarch, and to a significant extent the favorites were managed by a not-unknown 'bureau,' not infrequently by means of blackmail." And the professor writes further: "The person heading the church, Patriarch Pimen, by virtue of his inactivity, colorlessness, and lack of will was a very good match for the person who headed the state and the party. Even the corruption surrounding Pimen was well matched with Brezhnev's."

"The past decade" here is completely inaccurate. One has to speak of the past four or five decades. The professor is simply sacrificing the late patriarch in order to deflect criticism from the system.

For many years the state repressed the church not only administratively, but also economically, and our hierarchs actively helped the Soviet bureaucrats. One means of repression was the notorious "fight for peace," an aspect of which I will describe here:

In 1979 they ordained me and sent me to a poor village parish in Belgorod oblast'. I had served in the parish in Korovina for two weeks when I was ordered to appear with the churchwarden in the office of the secretary of the Volokonov raion executive committee. We went there, we both sat at the table silently, and the boss of the office – a well-groomed, impressive man – unhurriedly strolled back and forth; then he patronizingly filled us in, condescendingly outlining for me the subject matter of the major sermons, explaining to the churchwarden that the church should be run only by him, the churchwarden, and that the senior priest of the parish is no more than a hired laborer, a person who carries out orders. Then he went to the safe, took out a roll of white paper, and slowly and solemnly spread it out on the table before us. Covering the entire sheet of paper was a picture of L. I. Brezhnev on a platform, on his chest the stars of the Hero of the Soviet Union, his hand raised, calling us to fight for peace. A month had not passed since the introduction of a limited contingent of Soviet troops into Afghanistan.

"We think," the secretary pontificated, "that the Orthodox Church together with all the rest of the Soviet people is actively fighting for peace throughout the world. Pimen, the patriarch of all Russia, has written and spoken very eloquently about this. Our government not only does not stand in the way of this noble mission of the church, but approves and supports it to the utmost, and promotes the further development of the peace-making efforts of the church organizations and, especially, the growth of the ecumenical movement. Several years ago in Belgorod there was a special meeting of believers of the Orthodox, Baptist, and other denominations, where a decision was made that all the religious communities of the *oblast'* would contribute no less than 15 percent of their total income annually to the Peace Fund. The most progressive and politically conscious even give 20 percent. Certificates of honor and even government awards are bestowed upon the churchwardens and senior priests of such progressive communities. Well, your church is poor, so we will meet you halfway; for the time being you can contribute only 10 percent of your annual income to the Peace Fund." And he beamed happily at his own generosity.

The churchwarden started to wail that we were very poor, that we urgently needed to buy and transport construction materials, including bricks, cement, and galvanized iron, because soon it would be the building season and then nothing would be available. All the work in the parish was urgent, he said. "It's necessary to put on a new roof this very summer, to put down new floors, to plaster, to paint, to put up a fence, a barn, and a toilet, and there's not a cent in the cash box, there's nothing to pay the priest's wages – 100 rubles – with. Have mercy, reduce the levy a little more."

The secretary stopped smiling. "If we all start to argue this way," he explained didactically, "mankind will be on the brink of the abyss. If the imperialists unleash a nuclear war, you won't hide in your toilet, and a new galvanized roof won't save you." He rolled up the poster into a tube and gave us to understand that the audience was at an end. And, having displayed his anger, he didn't bother to shake hands. We rose too.

"Forgive me," I said, straightening my skullcap and cassock, "when did that conference you referred to, the meeting of representatives of believers, take place in Belgorod? I'd like to mention it in the parish in one of the sermons. And there's something I need to clear up with Archbishop Khrizostom."

"The fight for peace," he answered even more sternly, "is one of the most important tasks of our entire foreign policy; it must not be underestimated."

"Excuse me, I know that. *When* was the meeting in Belgorod, and who conducted it?"

"I don't recall at the moment; I'll try to find out and let you know."

"I really wish you would find out and tell me right away; I can wait until the end of the workday. I'll explain why. First, they always taught us that contributions to the Peace Fund in any case can be only voluntary, that no one ever has the right to establish any fixed sums or percentages. Second, and this is even more important, in our country religion is the private affair of each citizen. Religious affiliation is not indicated in any official document. An individual is in no way obligated to tell or report to anyone whether he is a believer or an atheist. How did they choose the delegates for such a conference? For sixty years there have been no 'conferences of believers' of that sort in our country, nor could there be in principle, and suddenly – there's one in Belgorod!"

One thing led to another; we both got angry and started to shout, said a lot of rude things to each other, and fell out in a big way. Only two hours later, already on the way home, I grasped that I was the only one who got angry; he intentionally taunted me and I, like a carp, took the bait. All the cards were in my hands at first; he was well aware of that, but I started shouting – and lost.

Then the churchwarden began to cry on the train. "Now this plenipotentiary won't let our church have its way in anything, very likely, and they'll get rid of the parish and give me the sack in the immediate future. Father, they have all the power, you don't know yet. Don't argue with them and don't go to law with them; they do whatever they like."

The churchwarden wasn't crying for nothing. The church to which they had sent me as priest had been converted into a storehouse for threshed grain in the early 1930s. When the war started they took out the grain, and services were resumed. In 1965, services were discontinued again; they didn't provide a priest, but the parish was still registered as active. The years passed, part of the roof was torn off by wind, the churchwarden died, the keys were kept by whoever was at hand, and then they stopped locking the church at all. Absolutely everything was stolen from it; only the bare walls were left, from which the plaster was falling in layers. They broke the windows, someone managed to make off with several frames, and the fence had been pulled down even before the war. But by some miracle the churchwardens of Korovina, Afonina, and Ivanovo got permission to resume services. True, they had to make more than one trip to Moscow for that purpose.

The church was not heated, and it was necessary to hold the service at temperatures of minus 15 to 18 degrees Celsius. Just try to hold first the chalice, then the metal cross in your bare hands. You can't hold the service in mittens. In summer the geese came into the church during the service, and for that reason the chickens came more rarely. The cows would look in the door, and swallows built nests in the anterior part of the church. A heavenly idyll, if you look at it that way.

According to the inventory of property that was compiled by workers from the raion financial department, the most valuable thing in the church was the Gospels on the altar, which they evaluated at eight rubles. In second place ranked the electric tea kettle, assessed at six rubles. And everything else, all thirty-four items of conservation, was valued at an average of between three rubles and one ruble, including icons of "unknown saints," "threadbare vestments," and other church equipment.

For the priest, there was a temporary shack like a piglet's little house, only the twigs weren't bare, but puttied with clay. The whole thing was scarcely bigger than a compartment in a railroad car; there was no way to house a family there. The raion executive committee would not allow another house to be bought in this or a neighboring village or a new one to be built near the church. We had requested it in vain for two years. "So, there's money for a house, but not for the Peace Fund? Bring it and give first to the Peace Fund." It was easy to find a reason for an official refusal, a very simple reply: The *kolkhoz* (collective farm) is growing, it needs living space badly itself; the *kolkhoz* itself will buy any house that is put up for sale within its territory. To whom should we have complained about such a refusal? Several times I wrote to Belgorod and explained that there was no lodge; they let it, together with the fence, go for use as road-surfacing ballast before the war; permit us, I asked, to rebuild with our money what you senselessly demolished. But the authorities didn't favor us with a reply.

In spring 1980, we began to put on a new roof, repair the cornices, and change the frames in the eight-faceted, prismatic part of the tower. The old grandmothers, coming to the service, would bring things in bags: one, a couple of bricks, another, a saucepan of cement. And the village soviet and the raion executive committee started to play dirty tricks with all their might: they refused to authorize documents for the churchwarden when we had to receive freight by rail, and the railroad can impose a huge fine for failure to unload the freight cars within the time agreed. For a long time the authorities refused to register the church's agreement with the roofers, and they insisted that it was impossible to start the work before registration, although the church was not listed as a monument. They refused to let the *kolkhoz* give us a vehicle, even though there was no transportation agency in Korovina. They sent a district policeman and ordered him to kick the roofers out: "Pay into the Peace Fund."

"The roofers work on credit," we explained, "they have agreed to get paid in the fall or even at the end of the year, the priest is going without his pay for several months, and everything has been spent on building materials."

"We don't know anything about that; put something in the Peace Fund!"

And never a day of rest, at every step and in every possible way they wore us down. On one of the holidays the churchwarden fell to his knees in the middle of the church and began to lament plaintively: "Father, they have pestered me to death, it's better that we stop the repairs. Just give your blessing to a donation of 100 rubles to the Peace Fund; otherwise they're threatening to close the church by year's end."

I can assure those who want to feel sorry for the churchwarden or me, those who want to charge the impressive secretary of the raion executive committee with something: we're talking about an ordinary priest in an ordinary village parish, an ordinary churchwarden, an ordinary bureaucrat, no worse and no better than any others. In Valuisk raion, which adjoined ours, the authorities also refused long and stubbornly to allow the reroofing of the church in Urazov; they raked money into that same fund with an iron hand, only that parish was much richer than ours, and they bought themselves out of trouble. Then they transferred me to the diocese of Vologda, but little changed with my move from south to north.

Since 1988, I have been serving in Kostroma diocese. My first church here was in the village of Ushakovo. A little more than a year after my appointment to this parish, I received a letter from the governing Archbishop Iov, for many years the deputy president of the internal church relations section of the Moscow Patriarchate. Several months before this he had been appointed to our diocese to replace Archbishop Kassian, who retired on account of his advanced age. There's no need to open or read such letters; almost all letters from the spiritual and secular authorities are about the same thing: Give money! Give more! Games of the state machinery, transfers from one posting to another, and money – that's all. Apparently nothing else interests the members of the higher orders of the clergy; dogma, the canons, and the liturgy are nothing more than "old clothes," in the expression of a fellow clergyman.

July 8, 1989, No. 338

Moscow Patriarchate

To All Fathers, Senior Priests, and Parish
Councils of the Diocese of Kostroma:

Beloved Fathers, Brothers, and Sisters in Christ!

Rendering thanks to God for His constantly manifested, all-bountiful mercy on all of us, I sincerely thank all the clergymen who earnestly show pastoral concern for the edification of their parishioners and also, together with the parish council, care about the splendor of their churches.

At the same time I am informing you that in July of this year, at the invitation of our church, meetings of the Central Committee of the World Council of Churches and a number of the committees associated with it will be held in our country for the first time. About seven hundred persons from almost one hundred countries will take part in these meetings, as well as translators and other personnel.

For our diocese of Kostroma there is an additional common concern – the construction of a new building for accommodating the services of the diocesan directorate and the archiepiscopal residential and official rooms, the realization of which we have already begun. We have yet another general concern, about feasible assistance to newly opened churches in our diocese and newly opened monasteries of general church significance, along with other charitable measures. The realization of all these measures requires huge financial outlays, both from the Moscow Patriarchate and from us.

Therefore I am turning to you, dear fathers, brothers, and sisters of the diocese of Kostroma, with a request. I as archbishop give my blessing to your attempt in every parish, starting with the second half of the current year, to find it possible to deposit most generous sums, payments for the proposed project, into the account of the Kostroma Diocesan Directorate for distribution to the proper quarter.

With Love in Christ,

Iov, Archbishop of Kostroma and Galich

Placed into the envelope together with the archbishop's blessing and with brotherly love was also a biting viper – the ruthless project estimate. Our parish would receive a blessing for donating 1,250 rubles, almost one fourth of its annual income, to the heretical crowd known as the "World Council of Churches." Another fourth would go for the usual diocesan payments, fees for candles, little icons, and other equipment, for ground rent, for insurance for the church building. Another fourth would go to pay the priest's wages. The remaining fourth would be spent on firewood, electricity, minor ongoing repairs, and the wages of the *dvornik*, or porter. That was the entire estimate of our expenditures, down to the last penny.

And then another functionary, the *oblast'* plenipotentiary of the Council for Religious Affairs, who will not be outdone by the archbishop, does not want to eat his bread for nothing. He wrote a letter and also sent it to all the parishes of the diocese. In it he also "sincerely thanks but at the same time informs that . . ." and "turns to you with a request to find a possibility." To put it bluntly, Give money. To the Peace Fund, to the V. I. Lenin Children's Fund, to the Charity and Health Fund. Sometimes we even gave on our own, without waiting for any kind of document – for example, after the earthquake in Armenia – but there's never any certainty that the money will reach its destination.

The church teaches us that repentance is the only path to rebirth to a new life; there has never been another way, nor will there ever be. It is never too late to repent, not for an individual, an entire nation, or a local church, as long as they still live. The thief repented even after he was hanging on the cross and suffering mortal torment, and that minute on the scales of divine justice outweighed his entire life. The prophet Jonah exactly predicted the day of the destruction of the huge city of Nineveh, but the people of Nineveh heeded the voice of the prophet and repented. "And God saw what they did, how they turned from their evil path, and God repented of the evil which he said he would do to them; and he did not do it" (Jon. 3 : 10).

And today all of us, every person, every nation know full well that the axe already is at the roots of the trees. But despite that knowledge, we, the Pharisees and Saducees of today, a breed of vipers, close our eyes and stop our ears. We set all our hopes not upon repentance and, through it, upon the spiritual rebirth of each Christian – and the rebirth of the entire Orthodox Russian Church and our entire fatherland – to new life, but upon external events and factors: political, economic, national, and cultural.

Alas, our cruel political, economic, and ecological ailments are merely a projection of our spiritual impoverishment into the sphere of politics and economics, into our perception of nature and the surrounding real world; they are merely symptoms of fatal spiritual evils. The church knows that but is silent; it hides its knowledge under a bushel, for today it too remains in voluntary sweet captivity.

This year too it is deprived of spiritual freedom to the same extent as in any of the preceding seventy years. Today too, our hierarchs are employed as court flatterers and panegyrists; throughout all the years they have never dared to say a word about the base conduct of the patriarchate, about the deviation into ecumenism and other forms of secular political maneuvering; they have not repented of their false witness against the new martyrs. Not a word of repentance has been uttered by the people who invariably helped the state of militant atheists to smother the church with levies beyond its means, forced donations to all manner of funds. Our hierarchs have not dared to speak, either to the people or to the government, about the fatal ailment of lack of spirituality that afflicts us all. Therefore all of us, Orthodox Christians and especially the clergy of the Moscow Patriarchate, are guilty of having brought our country to the brink of destruction. It is no longer the prophets, but the journalists who for a long time now have been crying out about the gulf yawning beneath our feet.

Every Christian knows that the physical recovery of a sick person begins with spiritual recovery and rebirth. As the Gospels recount, the paralytic first heard these words of our Savior: "Take heart, son! Your sins are forgiven." Only afterwards did he hear this: "Rise, take up your bed and go home" (Matt. 9:2–6).

The Christian way and Christian rebirth and renewal throughout all the centuries have been opposed by the anti-Christian way, known by various names such as "revolutionary reorganization of activity" or "the national patriotic movement." That way always seeks, and always succeeds in finding, external causes for any and all personal and national misfortunes and states of mind. The external enemy may be "the economic yoke of landowners and capitalists," "the international Jewish and Masonic conspiracy," "a band of hired saboteurs and diversionaries," or "Trotskyite-Zinov'evist rabble" – it is not important who or what; the pattern is eternally the same. What is important is the false message that there is nothing for us to be sorry for; it is not we who came to such a life, but they – the other people or circumstances – that brought us there.

But the future of Russia in the Time of Troubles at the beginning of the seventeenth century was decided neither in the political arena nor in the free market. Today too, our hope for salvation lies not in the bazaar of politics, nor in the economy, but in spiritual renewal.

THE ADVANTAGES OF EDUCATIONAL

FREEDOM NEW WINE IN OLD SKINS

ANDREI MAL'TSEV AND KIRILL NOVOSEL'SKII

Andrei Mal'tsev and Kirill Novosel'skii teach economics at the Ural State University of Economics in Ekaterinburg. Professor Mal'tsev, who heads the Department of Global Economics, is also vice-rector for International Affairs. Professor Novosel'skii is also a corresponding member of the Russian Ecological Academy. Here they discuss their fight for freedom of intellectual inquiry in their university, including efforts to improve the dialogue between Russian and Western economists.

Introduction

THE CHANGING OF political and economic realities in the late 1980s and early 1990s brought new hope and a new spirit to research and education in Russia. The case study we present here dates from that era of reform and involves a team of young academic researchers who began a new epoch in their careers by implementing dramatic structural changes in the traditional, Soviet-style school of economics in Ekaterinburg, formerly known as Sverdlovsk.

It is worth remembering that the Ural region, including Sverdlovsk *oblast'* (an administrative division of the country) and Ekaterinburg, its chief city, was a stronghold of the Soviet military-industrial complex, and as such it was closed to foreigners and isolated from most international contact. Even now there remain five "secret cities," several of them within the borders of present-day Russia, to which access is difficult, even for close relatives.

The policy of *glasnost'*, or openness, in the 1980s, the pro-market economic reforms of the 1990s, the development of strong and independent local authority, and the open-mindedness of our university's rector allowed us freedom in several areas: (1) We ourselves could formulate new fields of research and new subjects to teach; (2) Totalitarian control of the curriculum and methods of teaching came to an end; (3) New organizational structures were created within the university; (4) A multilingual approach to business education was implemented; (5) The quality of teaching was controlled independently by highly qualified faculty members; (6) In the teaching of international economic relations, ethical aspects were introduced; (7) Informal meetings – discussion groups, role-playing sessions, presentations by successful business managers, and the like – were instituted; and (8) Access to information from international sources increased as Internet resources were made available, study at foreign universities was allowed, and visiting professors from abroad were invited.

Let us describe our achievements and our fears step by step.

Philosophical Context

A sense of freedom never could have evolved from the ideology predominant in the Soviet Union in the 1970s and 1980s. That system of ideas had aggressively penetrated every pore of society, including the Soviet educational system. Access to older Russian liberal thinking, as well as contemporary Western philosophical writings, was limited. In those circumstances, only intuition and spiritual inspiration could help.

Philosophy still mattered, however. Andrei Sakharov's convergence theory and Nikolai Roerich's "peace through culture" concept certainly influenced us. The dissident academician Sakharov taught that at the end of the day, technology and common challenges would bring together the peoples separated by the Iron Curtain. This major contributor to the Soviet hydrogen bomb project placed ethics ahead of progress and, almost entirely on his own, worked untiringly to advance the human rights movement. In his book *Anxiety and Hope*, a collection of previously banned articles and speeches, Sakharov shows himself to be an optimist, a prophet, and a strong defender of what he describes as an interconnected triad: technical and social progress, peaceful coexistence, and intellectual freedom. Overcoming the splintering of the world into antagonistic groups of states, strengthening the role of international organizations as spokespersons for all human interests, promoting freedom of movement on our planet, and encouraging convergence of legal and economic rules and standards in different countries – these and other concerns of Sakharov's inspired us to instill a new spirit into the teaching of international economics.

Another idea of Sakharov's that proved fruitful in our creation of new courses – in economic geography, in this case – was the notion of delimiting two zones on earth: working areas and reserved areas. Working areas, major in terms of population but minor in terms of territory, would be regions of artificial landscape suited to human needs. By contrast, vast reserved areas would be left, he proposed, in order to preserve the balance of nature, provide recreation, and restore balance to human bodies and minds. Only in Rio de Janeiro in 1992, eighteen years after Andrei Sakharov expressed those ideas, did "sustainable development" become a central component in an international treaty.

Another cornerstone was provided by Nikolai Konstantinovich Roerich (Rerikh), a Russian-born painter, linguist, and philosopher who also devoted some thought to economics. In his essay "The Freedom of Goods," he urged, "Let goods live their life, move freely, and implant new qualities in those localities where they are of critical importance." And, more specifically: "How funny are all duties, barriers, and limitations – especially where the human mind was a creator!" Education is not an analytical process, he believed, but a synthetic one of seeing the relationships between things, perceiving the similarities rather than the differences. A teacher must maintain a free mind and "stand aside and not obscure the sun," as Diogenes requested. Because a teacher's task is to bring students to an awakening, he must teach only fundamental principles and let his students discover the details for themselves, Roerich thought.

Human progress is greatly dependent upon the work of pioneers, individuals who, not satisfied with the existing order, seek to discover new worlds and lead humanity into new fields of thought. Most people make the conservative choice to keep to the well-trodden paths of the past. As the Belgian writer Maurice Maeterlinck said, "At every crossroads on the way that leads to the future, each progressive spirit is opposed by a thousand men, appointed to guard the past."

Enlightening people by opening and guiding their minds is of primary importance to many great personalities, including successful businessman and philanthropist Sir John Templeton. We are newcomers to his ideas of achieving personal growth and prosperity, but we believe they will be useful in teaching the Russian business elite, including our students. Such principles as thankfulness, gratitude, prayer, forgiveness, and, especially, positive thinking can help in our work, though we must first adapt those concepts to the peculiarities of Russian psychology. More effort probably is needed to explain those moral principles in our country than in the West. Sir John Templeton teaches, for example, that "A real economic healing activity is to tithe, or give. It is found that tithing establishes a consistent method of giving and stewarding the bounty in one's life. Through this we increase our awareness about supply, abundance, and further giving. One can observe that the family that tithes for more than ten years becomes both prosperous and happy!" In the Russian cultural environment, it is necessary to cite the Bible extensively and carefully and to explain in detail the term "tithing" as the giving of at least one tenth of one's earnings to churches and charities.

This, then, is the philosophical context of our strong belief that freedom of academic inquiry and freedom of teaching are critical issues for universities at this juncture in our history. Other grounds for that belief lie in the peculiarities of the environment in our country.

Challenges of the Environment

The Ural State University of Economics is a major business school serving this entire economic region. Its five thousand students come from eight provinces in Russia's industrial heartland, an area known for several reasons: its early industrial heritage, its reputation as the country's military stronghold, and its abundance of dangerous and highly pollutant industries. Only in 1991 did the area begin to be opened to the outside world. Dozens of cities and towns there remain closed to the public, however, and as many as one million of its citizens live in isolation from major global trends.

Those circumstances make it even more difficult to implement modern business standards in the Urals, at the far eastern fringe of European civilization. Fear of becoming too open and vulnerable to foreigners, strong attachment to traditions of decision-making by a central government, and other characteristic attitudes in this region have to be taken into account.

The breakup of the Soviet Union, Russia's turn toward democratization and economic liberalization, and a revolution in mental attitudes (even if in only one of every one thousand people) made it possible for the teaching staff at our university to bring a young and talented generation face to face with European and global values. In the early 1990s, it was relatively easy to do away with the old-style curricula and start lecturing "live," using foreign media reports, data from international governmental and nongovernmental organizations, and information provided by guests from abroad. In the mid-1990s, many joint ventures with leading global firms were established in the Urals, and British and American Consulates General were opened, along with their informational, cultural, and business consultancy centers. The House of Friendship made an about-face, going from holding narrowly focused meetings with Communist allies to organizing informal and crowded receptions on every important occasion in dozens of foreign countries.

The period of the late 1990s was marked by a major technological breakthrough: the Internet. All our educational and research institutions, public libraries, many businesses, and many ordinary citizens are now networking on a global basis. Even the "secret cities" have limited access to this unlimited flow of ideas and information. Multicultural and multilingual approaches to understanding global political, social, and economic trends are top priorities in our university's methodology of teaching.

In our introductory course we now teach first-year students how to search for necessary information, process data, and make presentations. Keeping in mind our students' future need for employment, we organize excursions to, and round tables at, a number of the businesses registered in Ekaterinburg.

In "The Global Economy," one of our major course offerings, we try to present an accurate, up-to-date picture of the contemporary world in its industrial and regional dimensions, including the latest global trends made known to us by international economic organizations. Closer acquaintance with those international bodies and the ethics of dealing with them are the subjects of our course "International Economic Relations."

We try to get the fourth-year students practically involved in establishing useful and stable business contacts with partners abroad. Actually or virtually, via the Internet, they travel to worldwide destinations, absorb different business cultures, and become ready to work as members of a team.

Unfortunately, many of the events of everyday life conflict with this idyllic picture. There is environmental degradation; the living conditions of the majority of the population, including our students, are miserable; there is growing fear of a resurgence of Communism; and the authorities at all levels are impotent in their "fight" against criminal gangs. All this creates a widening, unpleasantly noticeable gap between the teaching of high moral principles and standards and the dangers of everyday reality. If coming generations are to save Russia and Eastern Europe from new turbulence, they will need open, practical minds. How, then, are we to create them?

Controversial Targets

First, in order to attract teens to our educational institution, it was necessary to introduce *new subjects* into the curriculum. And there were only a few people in the entire city who could immediately abandon traditional approaches to global political and economic realities and start teaching new visions. Students, teachers, and administrators all faced the challenges of envisioning a single world, rather than one divided into competing blocs; living in a shrinking country with a moderate level of development, rather than in an expanding superpower; and exercising personal self-determination, rather than accepting centrally planned activities. That list is far from comprehensive.

Who could start the dramatic transformation, beginning from such a low point? Would it be experienced teachers or independent-minded strangers? The university's board of governors invited our brand new team of investigators from the local branch of the Academy of Sciences to become involved. At that time, in 1992 and 1993, the team's members were just finishing their Ph.D. degrees. We had little interest in promoting ideological clichés; instead, we concentrated on expressing our own newly acquired knowledge. We didn't know the "right" way to teach certain things, but we were used to searching for alternatives, brainstorming "crazy" ideas, and finding logical, balanced solutions.

Luckily for the team, new gates were opened. Oddly, those gates looked wide and inviting to the participants, but seemed almost invisible to others. The new people were introduced one by one, indirectly, working for a few months in different traditional departments. Soon the team members were placed together, quite unexpectedly for the majority of the hard-liners. It is hard to imagine now what could have happened if our team had been introduced openly and in its entirety.

Many changes followed. Independent formulation of new areas of research and new subjects of instruction was allowed under the protection of the rector. Introducing a multicultural approach into the educational process, the chairman of the Department of Global Economics accepted the concept of a multipolar world based on a network of global cultures. Samuel Hantington's paradigm of the "clash of civilizations" was transformed into the concept of the "cooperation of cultures." Now our students of international business engage in role play, acting as representatives of European, Muslim, African, Latin American, Pacific, North American, and other global cultures.

Second, *new organizational structures* had to be created at the university. (See figures 1, 2, and 3.) Of historical importance for the university was the introduction of a new group of departments: the faculty of management and international economic relations. The founding members were the Department of Management, formed in 1991, and three departments set up in 1992: the Departments of Global Economics, International Trade, and Business Foreign Languages. The faculty members were young – 39.5 was the average age – and most spoke at least one foreign language. The Faculty of Management and International Relations and its Department of Business Foreign Languages remain unique; they are the only entities of their kind in the Ural economic region. Two-thirds of the teachers in the faculty hold degrees from another faculty.

During the past five years the university has become involved in providing a number of training programs for remuneration as part of the economic reform movement. Part of the money received goes to the teachers; part is used to renovate the facilities. Moreover, in the 1990s, a students' commercial bank, Vuzbank, became affiliated with the university, and students in the Department of Finance get practical training there.

The university has managed to retain contacts with experienced specialists and to develop new ties, and that achievement is especially important in the present situation. Previously the budget of an institution of higher education included funds to pay business consultants and others who could familiarize the students with aspects of business practice. Now nothing of the kind exists, but the ties remain intact. For example, the state examination commission in the Department of Global Economics has been chaired by a top executive of the Sverdlovsk *oblast'* administration and the Ekaterinburg city government: Mr. Sergei Vladimirovich Shapovalov, the chairman of the Ekaterinburg Municipal Committee on Interna-

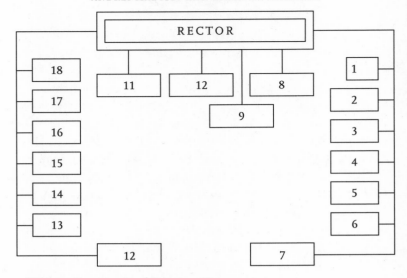

Figure 1. Organizational Structure Key

1 Legal Consultant
2 Academic Council
3 Scientific Secretary
4 General Supply Office
5 Degree-awarding Council
6 Engineer for Labor Security
7 Newspaper Editorial Board
8 Department of Political
   Economics
9 Council for Social Sciences

10 Department of Philosophy
    and Scientific Communism
11 Department of CPSU History
12 Administration Office
13 Accounting Office
14 Planning and Financial Office
15 Office N 2
16 Office N 1
17 Enrollment Board
18 Personnel Office

tional Economic Relations. In 1997, we formed the Alumni Association of the Ural State University of Economics, following the
model of Western universities. In light of the difficulties experienced in our country, the association is developing its activities
rather slowly.

The new approaches embraced by the rector and his team in the
early 1990s have produced results. Most important, despite the difficulties of the reforms, our university has not merely survived but
significantly strengthened its position and increased its renown.

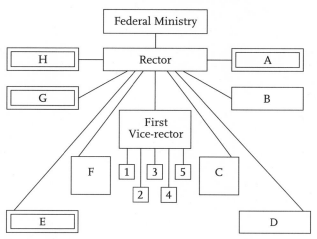

Figure 2. Ural State University of Economics: Structure in Mid-1980s

A CPSU Committee of the University
B Trade Union Committee
C Vice-rector for Scientific Research
D Vice-rector for Tutoring
E Vice-rector for Development
F Vice-rector for General Questions
G Young Communism League Committee
H Oblast' (City) CPSU Committee

The number of full professors at the university has grown from twelve in 1990 to the present total of forty-five. In 1994, it became the second of the fourteen state institutes of national economics in Russia to be granted university status.

It was the implementation of foreign-language programs for business use and the introduction of a multicultural approach that enabled the university to make a real breakthrough in upgrading the curriculum and improving the quality of specialized training. We hesitate to associate that major advance directly with the rector's decision to appoint the future head of the Department of Global Economics to the completely new post of vice-rector for International Affairs, but the facts speak for themselves. During the years

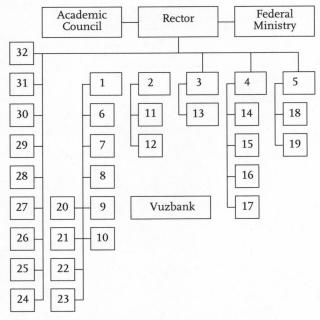

Figure 3. Present Structure of the Ural State University of Economics

1 First Vice-rector	16 Faculty of Distance Learning
2 Vice-rector for Science	17 Faculty of Advanced Learning
3 Vice-rector for International Relations	18 General Supply Office
	19 Sports Complex
4 Vice-rector for Tutoring	20 Curriculum Office
5 Vice-rector for General Questions	21 Library
6 Faculty of Finance	22 Computing Center
7 Faculty of Business	23 Publishing Office
8 Faculty of Engineering	24 Emergency Office
9 Faculty of Economics	25 Archive
10 Faculty of Management and International Economic Relations	26 Enrollment Board
	27 Accounting Office
11 Scientific Research Office	28 Job Promotion Office
12 Office of Postgraduate Education	29 Administration Office
13 Office of International Relations	30 Personnel Office
14 Museum	31 Trade Union Office
15 Institute for Continuous Learning	32 Military Recruitment Office

from 1992 to 1997, about ninety of our four hundred full-time teachers went abroad to participate in training courses of different duration, some lasting as long as a year. Their destinations included the United States, Great Britain, France, and Germany. Of the eighty teachers below the age of forty who occupy posts of senior instructor or higher, 50 percent completed a training course abroad during that period. Between thirty-five and forty-five foreign teachers, businessmen, and scientists attend our university annually.

There are two fundamental points here. First, it was a deliberate strategy of the newly appointed vice-rector for international affairs to provide the maximum number of training courses abroad to outstanding university teachers, especially young members of the faculty. It was necessary to quickly organize competent, active supporters for this new process of multicultural integration, since our university had never before known such a level of involvement in foreign study. We managed to cope with the problem. Participation in foreign training courses so far has resulted in two doctoral degrees, and three or four more dissertations will be finished soon.

Second, the financial aspect of foreign study deserves mention. Before the 1990s a teacher in an institution of higher learning could obtain an opportunity to study abroad only through the Ministry of Education. When reforms began, the opportunities available through the ministry decreased sharply. Of the approximately 130 trips made abroad by our teachers during the 1992–1998 period (many people went more than once), only seven were funded by the Ministry of Education. In most cases we used "alternative sources of financing" provided by international funds, foreign embassies, and various grants. It is a special pleasure to mention the establishment of long-term fruitful contacts with a number of foreign partners: the University of Akron in Akron, Ohio; the University of Wiesbaden in Germany; the Higher School of Commerce of the City of Pau, in France's province of Aquitaine; and the University of Northwest London, in Great Britain.

We remember with thanks the institutions and individuals that have helped us and still contribute to the development of such contacts: the U.S. Embassy in Moscow, in particular David Kennedy, formerly second secretary and later first secretary there; the U.S. Consulate General in Ekaterinburg; the Consulate General of Great Britain in Ekaterinburg; and DAAD, the German Academic Exchange Service.

Expected Obstacles

As a rule all the troubles and difficulties of any process fade from memory if the outcome is successful, since we tend to remember mainly the positive. At the moment we can hardly recall the details, though we do remember the most troublesome of the significant milestones on our way. The first step appeared to be the most difficult, for not one of the eight of us who moved to the university from the Institute of Economics, an affiliate of the Ural branch of the Academy of Sciences, had any teaching credentials. At the institute we had managed to build a promising, forward-looking team able to deal with numerous acutely challenging problems. It was evident that new problems required new people, but where would we find them? We ourselves had to become the problem solvers. In addition, we were motivated by the chance to engage in creative work in the favorable atmosphere promised us by the university's rector. That turned out to be crucial.

The most dramatic period was spring 1992, when the university's board of learning debated "to be or not to be" in regard to the faculty of management and international economic relations. Despite the rector's strong support, the board voted against the proposal. Only in late autumn 1992, after we had done the necessary preparatory work and established some personal contacts, did the board of learning approve the new faculty.

Actually, the entire period of the university reforms was intensely dramatic. Our university is a federal-level educational institution; that is, it is funded from Moscow. Recently, however, the Russian government reduced the funds available to us. Now state funds are intended to cover only student scholarships and the salaries of the staff and faculty members. Even worse, the university currently receives only one-third of the stipulated amount. The government allocates not a single penny for maintaining the grounds and buildings, updating the library's holdings, and the like. We try to earn the required amounts by providing the educational services mentioned earlier.

Competition in the educational services "market" is increasingly keen and fierce. That does not frighten us, but we insist that competition should be fair. When an academy of mining or an academy of railway transportation begins to educate lawyers, economists, and accountants, one has to wonder whether those involved in this "business" would consult a physician whose "diploma" was awarded, say, by an agricultural school. Surely, that is out of the question.

From the outset of our work, we heard incessant questions from people at our university who were venerable as to both age and position, people who never read a foreign newspaper or even spoke to a foreigner during their lives behind the Iron Curtain: "Why should the university have international relations?" "Won't these fellowships be a waste of money?" "What will these foreigners 'teach' us in the long run?" The last question proved to be the most enduring. We hope we have managed to dispel these doubts forever, at least at our university level, by holding numerous meetings and encouraging lively discourse with foreign lecturers. But we don't want our heads to be turned by success. Mutual understanding and reciprocal discoveries are long in coming, and tireless effort is needed to keep this avenue, with its two-way traffic, clean and open.

The Future

In summer 1998, we held our fifth graduation ceremony for students majoring in the field of global economics. About three hundred alumni of our program currently work in all the Ural regions and republics except Bashkortostan, in the administrations of the governors of Sverdlovsk, Orenburg, and Tiumen' *oblasts,* in a num-

Geographical Expansion of the Ural State University of Economics

ber of mayoral offices in Ural regional centers, in the largest export companies, in the leading banks, and in the local offices of well-known international companies. And they are doing good work. In autumn 1998, Maksim Deviatiarov, a third-year student majoring in global economics who works part-time in Coca-Cola's Ekaterin-burg office, was awarded a grant in recognition of excellent progress in his field of study. David Okenfold, general manager of Coca-Cola – Ekaterinburg, came to the city to make the award.

The faculty of management and international economic rela-tions has already celebrated its fifth anniversary. It is time to sum up our initial results. Chief among them is the fact that today it is next to impossible to mention the Ural State University of Eco-nomics without referring to this faculty. Assuming that Russia con-tinues its process of integration into the global economy, the de-mand for specialists able to work skillfully in global markets will be on the increase. The university's rector proved sagacious when, in the late 1980s, he first proposed introducing the study of global economics. It took two years to "push" the proposal in Moscow, in the Ministry of Education. Only in 1990 was approval granted. Our university, incidentally, was the first "peripheral" (outside Moscow) institution of higher education to receive such permission. Let us remind you that at that time both of us, as well as the rest of our future team, were still at the Institute of Economics, affiliated with the Academy of Sciences.

What are the prospects for our faculty and our university? Let us stress that higher education, despite all present-day difficulties, will remain an immutable value. To consolidate recent gains and provide a new generation with opportunities for a higher education of full value, however, certain factors must be present. We would like to point out three of them.

First, *the state's position on higher education* should be clear and firm. Here, keep in mind that private institutions of higher education in Russia recruit their teachers from state-owned higher schools; basically, they do not have their own permanent staff of qualified instructors. Thus they are not in a position to solve the problem of ensuring high-quality training for specialists. We are not opponents of paid higher education; we merely wish to raise the question of principles of state policy in the field of higher education. During the difficult years after World War II, the Soviet government found it possible to assign three times more of its budget revenues to the development of higher education than Russia does today. We are astonished by the attitude of those currently in authority who have reduced funding to 2 percent. Another illustration: the 50-percent drop in the USSR's industrial production during World War II was made up quickly, within a five-year period. Unfortunately, industrial production in Russia again is sharply declining. The present government should keep in mind the correlation between revitalization of production and investment in higher education. Moreover, active government support of science and education in the 1950s yielded world-renowned achievements by Soviet mathematicians, physicists, and space researchers.

Second, our *institutions of higher education* need to develop their own potential. In our university we happily note the growth of competition among applicants for admission. In some departments there are seven or eight applicants for each vacancy. The university-wide average is roughly 3.5 applicants per slot. Competition for admission to postgraduate programs, too, is on the rise. Also important is the university's ability to deal with practical requirements during a period of change. Between 1991 and 1998 our school launched fourteen new specialties and departments, including studies in the fields of global economics, environmental economics, and health economics. The "fresh blood" – new professors and instructors who came during that period – was less than 15 percent of the university-wide total and roughly one-third of the total in our faculty of management and international economic relations. At the same time, the average age of instructors has increased slightly, from forty-six in 1992 to forty-seven in 1998, as it is increasingly difficult to persuade the young generation to enter the teaching profession. On January 1, 1999, the average monthly salary of an associate professor with an advanced degree in science was 920 rubles, or about $50, while that of a full professor was 1,200 rubles, or $60.

Third, success in the training of highly skilled, independent professionals able to adapt to new work conditions (and here we speak not only of economists and lawyers) depends greatly on the existence of *favorable international conditions* and stable, long-term contacts for our university. Only recently, because of the reforms in our country, did such relationships become possible. We need to strengthen them, so that we never again are isolated behind an "Iron Curtain."

We now are ready to lend further support to international joint cooperation, whether it takes the form of joint training, common research projects, joint production of textbooks, or joint guidance of graduate papers with teachers at the University of Lyon, in France. In the international arena our university has something to be proud of: three of our graduates are now being trained at our partner school, the University of Akron, in the MBA program. In 1998, our

Department of Finance, together with the School of Business at the Central University of Connecticut, for the first time in our school's history published a textbook: *Financial Decision-making in Business Management: Concepts, Problems, Situations.* Last year we invited Philippa Bell from the United Kingdom to deliver lectures on global economics and the EC economy, in English. This year we are looking forward to the arrival of a visiting professor from California.

We are well aware that this is only the start of a journey down a long and difficult road. Years will pass before the socioeconomic transformations now under way are irreversible. These changes are intended to benefit mankind, to promote the development of the human spirit. And while restoration of the Russian economy is in progress, interest in our country is likely to grow. We are convinced that joint efforts in the field of education are the best way to enhance this process of transformation and restoration. Over the long term, investment in education will produce signs of new vitality and promote prosperity not only in Russia, but in the rest of the world as well.

CONCLUSION

FREEDOM, RESPONSIBILITY, AND

THE FUTURE OF RUSSIA

JAMES H. BILLINGTON

James Hadley Billington was sworn in as the Librarian of Congress on September 14, 1987. He was educated at Princeton University and earned his doctorate from Oxford University, where he was a Rhodes Scholar at Balliol College. In 1973, after a distinguished teaching career at Harvard and Princeton, he was appointed director of the Woodrow Wilson International Center for Scholars. Under his directorship, eight new programs were established at the Center, beginning with the Kennan Institute for Advanced Russian Studies. A writer and historian, he is the author of Mikhailovsky and Russian Populism *(1956),* The Icon and the Axe *(1966),* Fire in the Minds of Men *(1980),* Russia Transformed: Breakthrough to Hope, August 1991 *(1992), and* The Face of Russia *(1998), the companion book to the three-part PBS series,* The Face of Russia, *which he wrote and narrated. He has accompanied a number of congressional delegations to the USSR and was present at the barricades in Moscow during the events of August 1991.*

THE WOMAN is scantily clad and pretty much alone in a very cold place. She is beginning to shiver, may soon fall sick, and could even go out of her mind. But, for the moment, she is still standing – although by and large standing still. Certainly not convulsing, screaming, weeping, even complaining.

The man watches from afar by a warm fireplace. He finds the picture of the lady unpleasant but not alarming – mainly monotonous, unchanging, kind of dull. He changes channels in search of more action, more fun. He is sitting on an easy chair, not working at a desk chair. His hand is holding a clicker, not a mouse. Nothing too active, let alone interactive, no listening to feedback. The man does not identify with that lady lost in a vast land – or even wonder who she really is.

A storyteller from a Muslim region of that land once wrote a work called "The Mother of God in the Snow," hinting that this lady might be Raphael's Sistine Madonna being brought as a post-war trophy from the gallery at Dresden where the size of the gauge changed on the train tracks from Russia to Europe. Russians historically used the stopover to look at that gallery while waiting to make their connections. Perhaps the lady came from that devastated gallery deep into the Russian heartland. A storyteller from a Jewish background described a woman in the gulag accepting a jailer's taunt to celebrate an Easter liturgy hip-deep in water that was slowly freezing.

But, the lonely lady may not be a holy woman at all but simply depleted Russia itself. The ending, after all, is feminine for the word *Rossiya*, which Yeltsin called out repeatedly in a wintry rally in Red Square not long after the fall of Communism. Perhaps that was the first time that he seemed to realize that he had little else to say. It was in her name that he stumbled into Chechnya for a second time and created a successor out of the rising chorus of extremist nationalist rhetoric that sometimes invokes the older, also feminine, name of *Rus*, giving naked power a garb of sanctity.

Whoever she is, the lady has been left very much on her own. The cold is bitter at times in the great space that covers half of Asia and more than half of Europe. To the man who is watching TV from afar, it is simply the empty half of both continents. The lady's sad story plays itself out quietly on some largely unwatched cable channel. The reception is poor, and nothing much seems to be happening from the point of view of the man in the warm house living in a virtual reality of his own creation.

At the beginning of this century, the great cold space known as the Russian Empire was coming alive spiritually. Vibrant centers of new hope had appeared in all of the three great prophetic monotheisms that rose out of the bosom and the covenant of Abraham.

Judeo-Yiddish culture was exploding out of the pale of settlement in the West, Islam was finding new vitality in Bukhara and Samarkand in the east, and there was a long delayed recovery by the creative thinkers and artists of Russia of their half-forgotten roots in Orthodox Christianity. The landlocked lady was slaking her thirst along the deep interior rivers of Eurasia, particularly the mother of them all, the Volga, flowing from north to south, even as its tributaries flow both west from Asia and east from Europe.

Perhaps the lady that began coming in from the cold at the beginning of this century was not a mother but a sister. There were then, it was sometimes said, not one but two tsars in Russia: a uniformed Nicholas II, exercising fading power in St. Petersburg, and a barefoot Leo Tolstoy, seeking elusive truth in the countryside. Tolstoy had a sister who became a nun in the women's branch of the monastic complex of Optina Pustyn, where the great seekers of the past century – Gogol, Dostoevsky, Tolstoy – had all gone for spiritual renewal. Nicholas's wife, Alexandra, had a sister, Elizaveta, who became, in 1918, one of the first of the "new martyrs" sanctified later for accepting death voluntarily in the name of a faith that the Communist regime was determined to eradicate.

Perhaps the lady is beginning to come in from the cold again now at the end of the century, guided by people like Sister Maria Borisova from Kazan', the place where Europe and Asia meet and where Tolstoy first discovered wisdom in the east before he moved west, only to see Gandhi take his ideas back east. Could it even be that the neglected Russian lady on the steppe is in some way the sister of the American man watching on the tube? Certainly, these two were quarreling for a long time until very recently, much the way willful young siblings do, bitterly and persistently, but without ever inflicting ultimate damage on each other. They are both exiles, not just from Eden but from Europe. One went east, the other west, but their two frontiers met just north of San Francisco at places still known as the Russian River and Fort Ross.

The dissenters, adventurers, and pioneers who went west to America fought a civil war but then rose up a giant new dome atop Capitol Hill to celebrate the saving of their union. This, the highest point in our center of government, was modeled on the previously constructed tallest building in Russia's capital, St. Petersburg: the great dome of St. Isaac's Cathedral. These were the first two domes ever built reinforced with iron. Unlike the Russian original, the American dome is capped by a statue of liberty, a woman symbolizing freedom, our great American ideal, the goddess that was celebrated even for a fleeting, unforgettable moment in the ultimate East: in the great square before the Forbidden City in Beijing.

Liberty is still alive, but shivering in Russia: the land of exiles, dissenters, and adventurers who extended Europe's eastern frontier into Asia all along the Chinese border and up the Pacific Coast and across the Bering Strait to North America.

What has been the history of lady liberty in Russia, and what will be the fate of freedom there? Is it just the plaintive lyric cry of a captive such as that which Prince Igor cries out in Borodin's operatic version of Russia's most famous epic: "Give me, give me freedom." Is it just a poetic fantasy such as that which the poet Khlebnikov wrote in the first flush of revolutionary optimism in 1917, just before the Bolshevik takeover and the civil war?

> Freedom comes in naked,
> Throwing flowers on the heart,
> And we fall in step with her,
> Conversing with heaven about her . . .
>
> May the people be sovereign always,
> Everywhere: here, there,
> Let maidens sing out from ornate windows
> Amid songs from ancient processions
> About our true and sun-worshiping
> Autocracy of the people.

Freedom, which entered Russian life naked and vulnerable at the beginning of the twentieth century, reappeared dramatically at the century's end. But is lady liberty still just the mirage she was for the poet: a collage of nostalgic images from a past that never was and of utopian fantasies about a future that was never meant to be?

Is Russia, because of its vastness and lack of natural borders, always fated to have an autocracy, even if it is an autocracy of the people? Long before freedom entered modern Russian history as *svoboda*, the western idea of freedom from arbitrary, external force – freedom under the alternative name of *volya* – had shaped, populated, and indeed colonized most of Russia.

Volya in Russian means both "freedom" and "will," suggesting, in effect, the unlimited right to do almost anything. The term was used in legal documents to describe the excessive liberties that tsarist Russia gave to the aristocracy and also to Cossack militias in the borderlands. Alas, the term was also appropriated by radical intellectuals in the late tsarist period to express the illusory hope that a violent revolution would bring everyone everywhere the same kind of unlimited freedom that Cossacks and aristocrats had enjoyed in their limited domains.

The pioneering party of professional revolutionaries in the 1870s, called Land and Liberties, *(Zemlya i Volya)* became the first organization in human history ever to adopt the word "terrorist" as a designation of pride and honor. Its successor party, People's Freedom *(Narodnaya Volya)*, assassinated the last great hope for liberal reform in Russia, Tsar Alexander II; Lenin's older brother became the last great martyr of this movement, helping incubate the totalitarian revolutionary revenge that Lenin led to power. The name of the organization is properly translated by the alternate meaning of the word *volya* as the "People's Will" rather than as the "People's Freedom." The climactic line in the scene where Boris Godunov goes mad in Russia's greatest national opera occurs when the Tsar proclaims that it was not he who killed the young prince but "the will of the people." This was an eerie anticipation of the name taken just four years later by the revolutionary organization.

The Russian revolutionary tradition mixed the idea of the liberated will with the mythic Western idea derived from Rousseau that there was in society a "general will" above all petty, empirically evaluated attempts to describe what people actually wanted in their own narrow self-interest. In practice in Russia, the general will was eventually transmuted into the will of a general – in fact, of a generalissimo, Stalin. The people's will became the willfulness of a dictator. There was no freedom in Soviet Russia from the all-pervasive totalitarian state, no freedom even to remain silent; but, if freedom was banished, so too was its indispensable Siamese twin of responsibility.

"It doesn't depend on me" was the great mantra of everyone in the Soviet system. Someone higher up was always responsible for taking care of everything and everybody, and the man at the top was never responsible for anything that went wrong with anybody. He always blamed some faction that had previously exercised his will but subsequently had to be purged as if in compensation. To gullible Western visitors, a Soviet leader would profess ignorance or point to alleged constitutional limits he was forced to respect. Those suffering within the system understood it all in terms of a *pogovorka* (saying) whispered to one another: "Kill your own to scare the others."

What was striking about the overturn of Communism in Moscow during those dramatic days of August 1991 was that the Russian people were simultaneously recovering both freedom and responsibility. People not only freely exercised their refusal to obey the orders of the Communist junta, they also experienced an unprecedented forty-eight hours of having to make moral choices for themselves under conditions where authority was uncertain and the outcome was unknown. One had to decide whether or not to go to the barricades, to declare for or against the *putsch*, to speak up or not to speak up at one's place of work, within one's family, to one's neighbors, even to one's self. They were discovering the first dimension of a new and richer kind of freedom, the interior freedom to make choices based on conscience, one's inner light, one's better self.

The high point of the rediscovery that responsibility goes with freedom came with the public funeral of the three young men accidentally killed on the second night when an attack on the Russian White House had been generally expected. Yeltsin addressed the parents of the three boys with the famous words, "Forgive me, your president, that I was unable to defend and save your sons." Someone who was not responsible was nonetheless accepting responsibility in a society where no one had accepted responsibility for anything. Such legitimacy as was established in the new order was based more on that assumption of freedom with responsibility, I believe, than on any of the constitutional or political measures that were subsequently taken.

The discovery of freedom with responsibility led consciously or unconsciously, for many at least, to the question of "responsibility to what or to whom?" Although it was little acknowledged in the reportage in the West, many Russians discovered during those seventy-two hours and in the period of change more broadly that preceded and followed the collapse of Communism, what we look on as the first freedom, the freedom to worship. The Communist Party of the Soviet Union was the first political organization to rule large numbers of people with the expressed purpose of destroying all belief in religion. The return to religion, at least in the formal sense of widespread baptism early in the post-Soviet years, meant that many Russians were discovering what can be described as the vertical dimension of freedom. Orthodox Christianity developed in Russia a peculiarly intense belief in the omnipresence of a vertical connection with God even in the most lonely places and in the midst of the most profound suffering. There had been more than enough of both in the Soviet era, and the rediscovery of that dimension to life continues to grow out of – and often beyond – the denominational confines of Russian Orthodoxy and even of Christianity.

But what about freedom in its horizontal sense, support for the classic right to control one's own time and space without outside interference so long as one does not inflict harm on others? What about the simple freedom from outside interference? *Volya*, that word meaning both freedom and will, is the only word for freedom that is found in Vladimir Dal's great nineteenth century compendium of Russian proverbs, and it appears more as a foredoomed hope than as a reality. Just consider some of the representative entries: "Freedom lies out there, fate rules here." "Freedom lies out in the field. Who owns the field owns the freedom." Lack of freedom, however, in the same book of proverbs was not seen as a casual thing in traditional Russia, as in the proverb "Poverty is no sin; lack of freedom is no joke."

There was as well, however, a positive aspect to this early word for freedom, and Dimitry Likhachev, the great historian of Russian culture and, in many ways, the conscience of Russia in the 1990s, described *volya* as meaning "free will plus vast spaces." This type of expansive freedom was thought to be particularly found in Siberia. It was there that people sought to escape from repression, to find a fresh start with a new kind of entrepreneurship, free of the legacy of serfdom, confronted only with natural challenges rather than with centralized repression. And, so it is that new social, political, and economic starts are being made today in many interior spaces of Russia. The economic freedom that is being discovered is not just individual freedom, but also freedom that is often expressed in voluntary cooperative organizations similar to those that developed on the American frontier out of sheer necessity. De Tocqueville noted in his *Democracy in America* that locally based cooperative organizations really made democracy possible on a continental scale, a possibility about which many of America's founding fathers had been doubtful.

New creative activity seems to be developing from the bottom up in many parts of Russia even as systems that function from the top down seem to be dysfunctional. The young generation of governors, mayors, parish priests, and the non-monetized, barter-based, often small and medium scale economic arrangements that have developed within the vast expanses of interior Russia may be changing that country at the grass roots level in ways that none of us can find terms even to describe. The psychological and material basis for genuine decentralization of political and economic power may, for the first time in Russian history, have some possibility of becoming a reality.

But, asks the man still watching television from afar, will decentralization not lead basically to disintegration and the creation of a new dictatorship simply to hold things together? Russian Times of Troubles generally end up with worse tyrants at the end than at the beginning. The false Dimitry was worse than the unfairly maligned Boris Godunov, and Stalin, of course, incomparably worse than Nicholas II. We will also be told of the many parallels with late Weimar Germany: inflation; a demobilized, unhappy, and underpaid vast military force; and a sense of national humiliation. Russia will not return to Communism but could spiral down into something not so far removed from the Milosevic regime in Serbia. If the West has trouble with his regime in a small country like Yugoslavia in the heart of Europe, how would a similar leader affect us in the heart of Eurasia within a country many times larger and with a massive arsenal of weapons of mass destruction as a leading source of export earnings?

There are enormous dangers of which our geopolitical establishment seems as strangely ignorant as our casual viewer still clicking around on the television screen. Geopolitical destabilization in the heartland of the world's greatest land mass would unleash all kinds of dangers. America fought four wars in the twentieth century, one way or another to prevent authoritarian power from consolidating itself in that landmass and marginalizing the more maritime, entrepreneurial, and open societies of which we are the principal leader and exemplar.

But it is not the dangers so much as the opportunities that we are most guilty of overlooking. There is an extraordinary opportunity, first of all, for the renewal of our own democratic experiment by greater contact with the experiment that is going on at a much earlier stage in Russia, Ukraine, and other countries of the former Soviet Union. They are experiencing – however turbulently – the discovery not simply of freedom in the exterior sense but also in the interior sense of freedom combined with and sustained by responsibility. After all, it is true of us as well as of the Russians: if free people do not find responsibility within themselves, it will eventually be imposed on them by somebody else. Democracies have a deep, continuing need to reinforce legal with moral authority.

We have more of a stake in the Russian experiment in democracy than we tend to realize. In Russian history all the great changes have come about under the heavy influence of whomever was the principal foreign adversary of Russia. Russians raided Byzantium for many years before adopting Byzantine religion and culture. They fought the Swedes for a long time before adopting, under Peter the Great, a Swedish form of government. Even as they were resisting Napoleon, the French aristocracy sunk into French ways ever more deeply. As they were preparing to fight the Germans twice in the first half of the twentieth century, the Russians largely adopted the German method of large-scale industrial organization. We were the great adversary that they were seeking to "overtake and surpass." Now we are their main model for building a continent-wide federal democracy in a multi-ethnic country.

The two of us as nations were long the two scorpions in the nuclear bottle. Now that we have transmogrified out of our scorpion state, we seem incapable of handling the much lesser expense involved in starting joint enterprises and fresh undertakings for the human adventure.

I have two positive suggestions. It has often been said that money given to the central authorities somehow never reaches its ultimate destination. There are obvious remedies that involve more human involvement directly on the spot. But, there is a desperate need for Russians to see some home-grown examples of productive capitalism as distinguished from the conspicuous consumption capitalism that has been so much on display both on the awful television that we export to them and in the behavior of their own crony capitalists. It would be marvelous to have some pilot projects mounted in the interior – particularly in Siberia. I accompanied a delegation of senators a couple of years ago who were fascinated by Siberia, and two years ago the Congress gave the Library of Congress money to do a "Meeting of the Frontiers" project. We have already digitized and put on line the first pictures, maps, and documents recording the parallel experiences of the Russian expansion east and the American expansion west. This is our first bi-national project for the Internet, where we are already getting four million hits a day. There is now a developing network in Russia, and we hope that this will be a helpful way of dramatizing the commonalities between our two countries and also directing Russians away from their traditional approach to history into imaginative thinking about the development of their own country. But we have an obligation, it seems to me, and an opportunity to invest in some productive projects that will show creative capitalism at work on Russian soil, helping and working with them in a cooperative way.

A second thought is prompted by the fact that eventually everything comes back to politics in Russian-American relations. The people who are politically active in Russia today are very fluid in terms of allegiances, ideologies, thinking. They should all at least have an opportunity to see for themselves how an open society works. One-and-one-half percent of the Marshall Plan was spent on bringing young Germans over to America after the war. There is a big difference between the Russian and German situations, but the general principle is the same. We should not be lecturing to people who are ingenious and who have done so much with so many problems as have the Russians. Rather we should be sharing with them our own experience so they can take back for themselves impressions and ideas based on their own experiences rather than on someone else's lesson plan. They should particularly have that opportunity during the period of new leadership that will determine the legitimacy of the Russian system, probably for some years to come.

The Congress initiated just such an effort in 1999 by creating in the Library of Congress a Russian Leadership Program, which brought 2,150 emerging young political leaders (average age: 37) to America for intensive ten-day visits. They came from eighty-three of the eighty-nine political divisions of the Russian Federation and stayed for the most part in private homes in forty-five of the fifty states, seeing how the political system works in the context of our market economy and civil society. Though in some respects tensions deepened in the wake of Kosovo and Chechnya, new and younger leaders came into power in the Russian elections, and this remarkable program was renewed by the Congress for the year 2000.

In both the television series and the book that I recently wrote under the title *The Face of Russia*, I try to remind Western audiences of one very simple but forgotten fact: Russians have an enormous proven capability to be suddenly creative, precisely in areas with which they have no prior experience. In the case of painting, they suddenly adopted lock, stock, and barrel Byzantine iconography but then did something wildly original with it before it broke down under the spell of naturalism. In a much more shortened time span, they went through the same cycle in architecture, writing, music, and cinema. In all these great artistic media, the Russians displayed what the great cultural historian Yury Lotman, in his last posthumous book, called "a culture of explosion."

They tend to do something suddenly and creatively in an area in which they have had no previous experience. Tolstoy, Dostoevsky, Turgenev, and a whole host of other novelists produced one of the greatest explosions of novel writing at precisely the time that many critics in France and Britain and Germany were saying the novel was finished and no one could possibly say anything new. Yet, suddenly, in a medium where the Russians had little prior experience, there exploded enormous creativity.

No one expected the great events of August 1991. The conventional wisdom that everyone seems to accept passively now is that Russia will need twenty to thirty years to sort it all out. This seems to me much too pessimistic. There is no certainty, but there is a proven record in other areas of creativity. If creating a constitutional rule of law to protect freedom is a work of art, not science, then the experience of Russians with other art media gives one hope that they may display a perhaps hitherto not yet fully demonstrated ability to produce suddenly something positive in the political sphere more rapidly than any of us presently has had reason to hope.

On the eve of *perestroika* and the great changes, one of the most comprehensive one-volume studies of Russia ever produced in this country was published by a wide range of experts from a full range of disciplines and methodologies. They indicated that the only thing they all agreed on was that the Soviet system would remain basically unchanged for many years. No sooner was the print dry than the changes had begun. It may be too much to expect still more dramatic changes, but the variety of inventive testimony given at the Templeton Conference in the Library of Congress in February 1999 from different parts of Russia and the enthusiastic response of 2,150 young Russian leaders to their 1999 visit to America under the Library of Congress's auspices both give some grounds for hope. Anyone who surveys the richness and variety of unexpected leaps that this people has been capable of in other spheres should be hesitant to predict that Russians will not be successful in new spheres where an experimental spirit of innovation is needed. All of us trying to preserve the democratic rule of law and the moral and spiritual roots that underlie it have a deep stake in the effort of young Russians to enshrine these forces in the Eurasian heartland.

The lady out in the cold is our sister. We, as well as they, will be deeply impoverished if lady liberty on the dome of our Capitol cannot be, if not on the top of St. Isaac's, at the top of the list of accomplishments of the Russian people, as they and we enter the new millennium.

APPENDIX

SEVEN STEPS TO PROSPERITY

IN RUSSIA

The manifesto below was circulated in Russia among members of the Federal Duma and the international investment community in 1999; it was placed in the public domain without copyright or attribution. This document, which offers a number of very practical and insightful perspectives of relevance to the future of freedom in Russia, is presented here as an important and succinct summary of the core issues of reform facing Russians today. Preceding "Seven Steps" itself is the cover letter used when it was distributed in Russia.

Respected Duma Member:

Russia needs moral reform, not only economic reform.

Today the Russian people are at a crossroads in the development of this great nation. There is no way back, yet the way forward seems uncertain.

Courageously, the nation embraced many difficult reforms, and thus the seeds of a prosperous tomorrow were sown – so why has the crop of our prosperity failed? It is said that the economic reforms failed. But let us be honest: Weren't the young shoots of economic growth choked by the weeds of short-term self-interest as people at all levels seized what they could, regardless of the interests of others?

Even the best economic plan is doomed to failure if everyone, low and high alike, is committed to abusing the system to achieve self-enrichment. Whether this be accomplished by stealing assets, offering or accepting bribes, or evading taxes makes little difference. Let us be honest enough to admit that our dysfunctional economic system is not a viable economy at all. This system cannot take our country to the levels of wealth and prosperity enjoyed by other leading economic powers. It is based upon uncontrolled cronyism and corruption; its citizens tear from each others' hands the shattered fragments of the Soviet state.

Russia needs a program of moral reform, not only economic reform. To harvest a great crop, the soil must first be prepared: let us plow up the old thinking of each person, group, and faction seeking its own interest before that of its neighbor. Let us create an effective mechanism of distributing wealth and find the discipline to employ it with respect for our nation and its laws. If the nation now fails to build a civil society that respects the rights of each person, then the harvest of the future will be such wrenching strife that the remaining fabric of our society will surely be torn apart. Certainly, let the wisdom distilled from the experience of other nations guide us in building the new system, but let us also have the discipline to plow a straight course and refrain from indulging in today's temptations at the expense of tomorrow's growth.

The ideas expressed above are obvious and familiar, but how difficult it is for each of us to follow simple moral principles when everyone around us apparently has abandoned them. Which of you does not remember those moments of despair when your personal attempts to make a difference in your own sphere collided with the outrageous inefficiency of the current system, when you needed to scale the walls of bureaucracy, indifference, incompetence, and self-interest in order to accomplish any task? But who, if not you, has the power to start acting in accordance with your true principles, here and now? Leadership offers a unique opportunity to make a difference in the moral foundations of society. Remember the sense of appreciation you had whenever you encountered examples of integrity among civil servants and businessmen. Imagine what a difference you could make to people if they saw your behavior as another such example.

In the wake of the current crises, a group of concerned individuals have taken the time to produce "Seven Steps to Prosperity," a manifesto for these challenging times written by ordinary people.

Please take some of your valuable time to read through this document. Its ideas are not new, and they belong to all of us. We urge you to consider the "Seven Steps," to add to their number, to make them your own, and to seek ways of encouraging their implementation.

We cannot afford to fight amongst ourselves any longer. Fixing the roof does not help when the weak foundation can no longer stop the house from collapsing When the collapse comes, it is a tragedy for all, landlords and tenants alike, regardless of their principles and ambitions. It is time to gather the wonderful resources of Mother Russia and work together to build a common future, based on an integrity that will bring prosperity to all Russians. Prosperity is built on the cornerstones of honesty, fair dealing, and societal morality; without them, the commonwealth is doomed to destruction. Each of us has an opportunity to contribute to the solution. It is time for a prosperous Russia to take its rightful place in the world. If we persist in doing what is right, we will surely reap our harvest in due season. But are we willing to make sacrifices and work together now?

I am the chairman of a Western company that has invested in Russia since 1994. These issues have been discussed with other foreign investors, as well as with representatives of the World Bank and the EBRD. Though they agree with these views, they clearly are not in a position to make the changes that are necessary. That is why I am writing this letter to you.

Yours truly,

RUSSIA: SEVEN STEPS TO PROSPERITY

1. Tax Code

Make the code simpler, fairer, and more efficient. Reduce tax rates across the board to encourage payment. Improve the tax collection infrastructure through use of up-to-date computers to track taxpayers and payments. Shift the tax base to a focus on consumers and profits, rather than turnover and payroll taxes on industry. The tax system should encourage investment and efficiency. Barter must be eliminated.

Russian citizens need to believe that they are being taxed fairly and that the money collected will be spent wisely. A simplified tax system must demonstrate that everyone, including the privileged, is paying tax and that the tax burden is being fairly shared by each according to his ability to pay, without abusing the productive members of society through excessive or "progressive" taxation.

Simplest of all may be to adopt a consumption tax at a low, flat rate such as 15 percent. Such a tax would have the dual advantages of being easy to administer and encouraging saving and investment, since it would tax consumption rather than income. Because three quarters of Russia's citizens pay no tax, this would gently accustom the population to paying a small tax. Rates could be raised to European levels of 18 to 20 percent at a later date, as needed.

To encourage the payment of such a tax, Italy, which also has had problems with a large "parallel economy," developed a simple system whereby every transaction requires the issuing of a receipt *(ricevuta fiscale)*. The tax police perform spot checks of customers leaving shops to ensure that the receipt has been issued. Failure to produce the tax receipt makes both the purchaser and the shop liable to fines based upon a percentage of the transaction value.

2. Bankruptcy Law

There needs to be an effective bankruptcy law to establish the basis of a free market and to incline investment and human capital to produce goods and services for which a need exists. Further, an effective bankruptcy law is a prerequisite for sound and efficient banks and lending institutions.

Bankruptcy provides the ultimate form of accountability. It is axiomatic that actions have consequences, and in everyday life, consequences are the "feedback mechanism" that stimulates learning, correction, and progress. In the West, bankruptcy is always a last resort, and companies are encouraged to "work out" their difficulties if they can provide a plan demonstrating how they intend to meet their commitments. Given the massive dislocation that the Russian economic transition has engendered, there is a natural and magnanimous tendency toward forbearance where bankrupt organizations are concerned. Unfortunately, indiscriminate tolerance leads to a lack of accountability and demonstrates that no consequences ensue from inadequate performance or behavior. Russians must start to see that redundant and mismanaged organizations will not be permitted to consume society's scarce resources without having at least a reasonable prospect of generating a profit – that is, generating more than they consume. Unless bankruptcy provides a credible threat of accountability, demonstrated through initiation of bankruptcy proceedings, economic abuses will continue.

3. Investor Protection

Laws, regulation, and enforcement need to be reviewed.

(i) The regulation of protections for investors needs to be overhauled to achieve conformity with international standards and eliminate the abuses of shareholders' rights, which have discredited the market.

(ii) Grant the Russian SEC real enforcement powers, and make penalties severe enough to be a deterrent to abuse. Enact laws that guarantee investors transparency through good corporate governance.

(iii) The Russian stock market must be shown to be a regulated, transparent market where companies can come to raise capital and investors can be sure that their interests as minority shareholders are protected. Parastatal companies such as Gazprom and UES should be shown to be managed for all shareholders. Gazprom's two-tier share structure should be eliminated, as it allows corruption, creates confusion, and is inconsistent with free, open, and transparent markets.

(iv) Russian flight capital and private foreign capital will not return without new regulation to protect investors. If these funds return, they could be more important than IMF assistance and could dramatically reduce dependence on funding by external agencies such as the IMF, the World Bank, and the EBRD.

Many of Russia's major industrial and natural-resource companies are being plundered through the use of satellite businesses, owned by the companies' managers, which provide raw materials at inflated prices and purchase the finished goods at below-market prices. Such transfer pricing moves the profit from the core industrial business into the pockets of the managers. Consequently, no taxes are paid, there is no growth in employee wages, and, importantly, there is no return on the investment capital employed.

This "hollowing out" of Russian industry from the inside is further compounded where export businesses are concerned, as the operating profits of Russia's major exporters are easily transferred offshore through these management-owned companies. They accumulate in the managers' foreign bank accounts and deprive the Russian economy of much-needed capital and hard currency. This practice is employed by many of the exporters of oil, metals, and other natural resources. The enrichment of the few at the expense of the workers, taxpayers, and shareholders is criminal – it constitutes theft, tax evasion, and oppression of minorities – and ought to be treated as such.

The capitalist system cannot function without a return on the capital employed. The result of this widespread abuse is evident in the low rates of tax collection and in the faltering performance of whole industries, as managers hijack the businesses entrusted to them with impunity.

4. Banking System and Pension Plans

In order for confidence to return to the banking system, Russia must revise its banking regulation and institute professional oversight. Because of the lack of Russian expertise in banking, the market should be opened to foreign banks or joint ventures (with majority foreign ownership) to allow transfer of know-how, technology, and best practices. The population has lost faith in domestic banks.

A good comparison is Brazil, where over 80 percent of the banking system is foreign-owned. A sound banking system is a precondition, if Russians are to take the estimated $40 billion they hide at home and put it into banks where it can be used for investment and lending to industry. The development of private pension plans, as in Chile, would also provide capital to industry.

Russia lacks a basic banking industry. The term "banks," when applied to the investment banks/hedge funds of Russia, is misleading and a misnomer. The "Main Street" banks of the West are primarily deposit-taking, loan-making institutions. The Russian banks essentially have borrowed large sums to play the financial markets.

The skills and experience required for sound evaluation of loan applications are absent in Russia, and if Russian main-street banks were operating as lending institutions today, they would suffer significant, crisis-inducing losses through poor lending controls while they learned the business. The costliness of this learning curve has been demonstrated amply in other developing capital markets, in Asia and Latin America. There is a clear need for foreign retail banks to be given access to the Russian market. Institutions such as Hongkong Bank, Citibank, Barclays, and others would bring a skill-set of immense value and restore public confidence in this tarnished Russian industry. This could be seen as a beneficial form of "technology transfer."

5. Land Reform

Private ownership of land is the foundation of entrepreneurial and middle-class wealth in democratic countries. It gives people an incentive to work and build capital and encourages the efficient use of land. Residential mortgages are usually one of the foundations of the banking system, and the banking system in turn is a foundation of the services economy. People who own homes also invest in improvements, and such investment is also a major driver of economic activity in most developed countries.

Stable countries and economies need a significant middle class that will seek to protect the country's economic well-being and political stability. The right to purchase, develop, borrow against, and resell real estate is vital to the process of developing a strong middle class. In the West, the owners of many small businesses develop their seed capital through ownership and development of their own homes, shops, or farms.

It is difficult to see a surge in the number of small businesses, yielding a stable middle class, unless land reform enables Russian citizens to own their own homes, shops, and farms. A major secondary result clearly will be the more efficient use of all types of land, both agricultural and urban, as each landowner seeks to maximize the return from his "patrimony." The efficient use of farmland would reduce Russian dependence on food imports and create a dynamic farming industry. This could also significantly reduce "urban drift" from the farms – consider Chinese land reforms – and, in due course, become a revenue source for the state through the collection of land-transfer taxes. The benefit to the Russian economy would be real and demonstrable.

The challenge is to undertake land reform in such a way that the small landowner is not duped out of his holding by aggressive attempts to plunder the country, just as share privatization led to many Russian managers' "harvesting" the stock of Russian companies from unknowing workers. One way might be to privatize land and forbid the transfer of the title for three years thereafter. Inevitably, people would enter into "forward sale contracts," but the law could deter this by declaring all contracts having the effect of a forward sale to be unenforceable. Though somewhat draconian, this approach would be no worse than the existing situation, and it would allow landowners time to consider investing in their real-estate asset and enhancing its value.

6. Social Responsibility and the Development of Morality

(i) Develop a balance between social responsibility and economic development. Only a strong, vibrant economy will give the country the financial resources to build a fair and just social system.

(ii) Make corruption unacceptable. Promote ethics and values in government administration. This step is especially important in a country where religion has been banned for most of this century and where the moral foundation of the culture is weak. Many people have survived by circumventing rules under Communist governments. Many of today's problems can be traced back to this central issue: No value has been placed on morality in society. Russian culture must now evolve by incorporating a moral dimension if it is to justify foreign investment and support.

(iii) The rule of law needs to be established. The civil and criminal codes and the functioning of the legal system, the police, and the judiciary system should be reviewed. Often, laws exist but are not enforced. How many officials have been imprisoned for corruption?

(iv) Greater transparency is needed for people in fiduciary roles, such as public officials and corporate managers.

(v) Eliminate barter. Barter is the doorway to corruption; it puts temptation in people's way.

The fundamental problem is a moral one. Too many individuals abuse the system with impunity. Uninhibited self-enrichment is the name of the game, and too few people are willing to voluntarily respect the rules of the capitalist game: the rules of ownership, requiring proper corporate governance and transparency and entailing respect for minority rights; the rules of accountability, including observing the law, paying taxes, and telling the truth. Many Russians seem to see capitalism as an amoral system of "every man for himself." Perhaps this should not surprise us, given the Russians' experience under the Soviet system, where the top dog frequently used his position to garner the spoils. Under the Communist system, however, there were at least some checks and balances – albeit inefficient by Western standards – that ensured a basic degree of accountability to the community for the resources being consumed.

In the liberalized Russian system, a veneer of capitalism covers a rotten core of unchecked cronyism. It is a pity that too few influential individuals have sufficient economic incentive or moral fortitude to change the situation. As Steve Hanke writes, "Russia has entered a pre-Revolutionary political phase. The economy is neither a communist system nor a capitalist one, but that doesn't mean that it's in a period of transition: Russia has not been moving toward a market economy. Today, the Russian economy is a mutation of the old communist system and is totally dysfunctional."

The cronyism and uninhibited misappropriation of Soviet assets under the pretense of reform has given real capitalism a bad name. There may be a need to teach the Russian people that democratic capitalism is not "communism without accountability."

If citizens desire a free society, then they must be willing to support that society with integrity. That means choosing to obey laws, seeking the betterment of their fellow citizens, and creating an environment where business and productivity can flourish. Further, it means paying taxes to support law and order and fund public services. Such efforts must start at the top. Russia's leaders must look to themselves if they wish to improve the current situation. They must lead by example, pay their taxes, and eschew cronyism, graft, and corruption. The long-term solution might include a public awareness/media campaign explaining that capitalism must be built on pillars of integrity, accountability, transparency, and truth.

7. Restructuring the Domestic Debt

This debt must be restructured in a manner consistent with international standards of fair dealing, based on examples such as Latin America. Appoint a respected international investment bank or respected institution to broker a "Brady-type" deal acceptable to all parties that restores Russia's credibility. Russia must demonstrate the principles of fairness and equality of treatment if it is to recover some of its reputation as a sovereign borrower.

If Russia wants to access the international capital markets and attract investment, it must demonstrate that it plays by the rules of the international financial community. If Russia wants to be part of the global financial community, it must show that it can exercise the moral responsibility that accompanies this privilege.

GLOSSARY

CHEKA. Soviet security organ, 1918–1922.
Abbreviation of *Chrezvychainaia Komissiia po bor'be s kontrrevoliutsiei, sabotazhem i spekuliatsiei.*

DVORNIK. Porter; yardman.

KHOZRASCHET. Operation on self-supporting basis, cost accounting.

KRAI. Administrative area.

OBLAST'. Administrative division.

OKRUG. Administrative subdivision of republic, *krai,* or *oblast'.*

RAION. Administrative region.

SAMIZDAT. Illicit reproduction of unpublished material in the USSR.

INDEX

Index

Index

samizdat, 110, 179
Scalia, Antonin, 169
School for Advertising Agents, 152
scout troops, 121–23, 128
secret cities, 192, 196
sector theory, 155–59, 161
Seleznev, 53
separation of powers, 25, 29, 31–32, 132–35, 138
Serebrennikov, I. P, 28
Sergei, Father, 116–17
Seslavinskii, Mikhail, 149
"Seven Steps to Prosperity" manifesto, 225–34
Shapovalov, Sergei Vladimirovich, 199
Shchelukhin, V. V., 28
Siberian Center for the Support of Civic Initiatives, 158, 160
Siklova, Jirina, 157
Simanskii, Patriarch Aleksii, 179
small business, 71–79, 83–97, 102–103
Smirnov, V. A., 29, 41
social contract, 94–96, 139–40 (*See also* ethics)
Solov'ev, Sergei, 110
Solovieva, Alla, 161
Soros Foundation, 154
Southern Poverty Law Center, 100
Soviet Union, 5–9, 20–21, 41, 63, 99–102
speech, freedom of, x, 145–50
St. Isaac's Cathedral, 214, 223
Stalin, Josef, 61, 216, 219
Strathmore Paper Company, 80
Sushkov, O. V., 30
svoboda, 215

Talantov, Boris, 179
taxes, 12, 35–36, 56, 65, 73, 96, 149, 227–28
television, 144–49, 151–52
Templeton, Sir John, viii, x, 83, 195
Templeton Conference, viii, 223
theater, youth, 121
third sector. *See* nongovernmental organizations (NGOs)
time, concept of, 95, 103

tithing, 195
Tocqueville, Alexis de, 156, 218
Tolstoy, Leo, 222
trade unions, 156 (*See also* nongovernmental organizations (NGOs))
treason, 29
trials, public, 138
Tsar's Hunting Lodge (restaurant), 73, 75
Turgenev, Ivan, 222
tusovka, 109

universities: Akron (Ohio), 203, 208; Central, Connecticut, 209; Northwest London, 203; structure reforms, 199–203; Ural State, 199–206; Wiesbaden (Germany), 203
U.S. Immigration and Naturalization Service, 101
U.S. Information Service (USIS), 84
U.S.-Russian relations, 100–102, 218–21
USAID (U.S. Agency for International Development), 83–84
Uzzell, Lawrence A., 165

Vanden Heuvel, William J., vii
Varlamova, Natalia, 157
Vedernikov, N. T., 33
Velikhov, Evgenii, 85
Vestnik (journal), 177, 179, 181
VGTRK (All Russian State Television and Radio Company), 144
Viazemskii, Petr, 156
Vil'chek. V., 143
Vitruk, N. V., 28, 40
Voice of America, 165–66
volunteerism, 156 (*See also* nongovernmental organizations (NGOs))
volya, 215
voter education, 143, 151–52
voting rights, 37–38, 138
Vuzbank, 198–99, 202

White Sun of the Desert (restaurant), 74
World Bank, 50, 230